DENVER
BEER

DENVER
BEER

A HISTORY OF MILE HIGH BREWING

JONATHAN SHIKES

AMERICAN PALATE

Published by American Palate
A Division of The History Press
Charleston, SC
www.historypress.com

Front cover: Denver skyline at sunset. *Photo by Larry Johnson.*

First published 2020

Manufactured in the United States

ISBN 9781467139649

Library of Congress Control Number: 2019954256

Notice: The information in this book is true and complete to the best of our knowledge. It is offered without guarantee on the part of the author or The History Press. The author and The History Press disclaim all liability in connection with the use of this book.

This book is dedicated to my friend Will Pascoe, 1968–2018.

CONTENTS

PREFACE

I was born in Denver in 1969, the same year that Tivoli Brewing, whose roots go all the way back to the city's rugged beginnings, closed, ending a 110-year legacy. Denver was a different city back then—a cow town known mostly for Coors beer and its status as a flyover state. By the time I was eighteen, though, Colorado had changed. There had a been an oil boom, an oil bust, a skiing boom, a famous blizzard and, oh yeah, the Brown Cloud. And of course, there were the three famous Johns: John Denver, John Elway and, unfortunately, John Hinckley.

By 1987, there was also a thriving homebrewing scene, though only one microbrewery, Boulder Beer. That same year, a law that been in place since the end of Prohibition, more than fifty years earlier, changed. It raised the age at which people could buy 3.2 percent beer from eighteen to twenty-one but grandfathered in anyone who had already turned eighteen. So, if you turned eighteen before the cutoff date on July 1, as I did, you could keep buying 3.2 beer. But if you missed the cutoff, like my high school friend Patrick, you were out of luck.

Patrick wasn't the kind of guy who would let something like that stop him, though. Back then, he lived with his family in a house about three blocks from the Wine and Hop Shop, a homebrew store managed by a guy with, as I accurately or inaccurately remember, a big, scraggly beard.

Patrick and I walked over and bought the 1984 edition of Charlie Papazian's *The Complete Joy of Homebrewing*, which we read. Then we bought a carboy, a five-gallon white bucket, tubes, clamps, bleach, a hydrometer, an old-school bottle capper, a couple cans of malted extract, some hops, some yeast and some sugar. I don't remember the first beer we made, but over the next year, we cooked up a wide variety of Papazian's recipes—from Wise Ass Red Bitter to Naked Sunday Brown Ale, from Cheeks to the Wind Mild to Goat Scrotum Ale. We had a blast. How could we not? Two eighteen-year-olds brewing beer with names like Goat Scrotum Ale on their moms' stoves? Bliss.

More than that, though, it was the first time I tasted any of those styles. Prior to this, my liquid diet consisted of Coors, Coors Light, Coors Extra Gold, Miller Lite, Budweiser, Bud Ice, Milwaukee's Best, Stroh's and Meisterbrau. The fanciest beer I'd had was a Guinness, which a friend's father drank. My palate changed, and a lifelong interest was born. Although I'd continue to drink plenty of mass-produced light lagers, I also sought out whatever full-flavored beers I could find—from Pete's Wicked Ale to beers from Widmer and Red Hook, Blue Moon and Tommyknocker, Breckenridge, Left Hand and Wynkoop.

In the late 1990s, I discovered Sierra Nevada Pale Ale, and like a lot of people who drank that beer, I was never the same. Throughout my multistate career as a writer, editor and journalist, I continued to seek out bigger and better beers. Then, in 2007, I began my second stint as an editor with *Westword*, the alt-weekly newspaper in Denver. At the time, media companies were still looking for their voices online, and we were encouraged to find subjects to blog about. I realized that aside from two or three bloggers and an occasional column from the *Denver Post*'s Dick "Mr. Beer" Kreck, no one was writing about the state's microbreweries—now called craft breweries. So, I took it upon myself to start.

Boy, did that turn out well. Over the next decade, I watched as both Denver and craft beer exploded onto the national scene, and I got to write about every facet of it. Today, the city is almost unrecognizable from the town it was in the 1980s, and the beers, well, they have changed just as much. But the story of beer has always been one of change.

Writing this book made me realize how interconnected the city's history is with its beverage of choice. It's a story I hope you will enjoy as much as I do.

ACKNOWLEDGEMENTS

I needed a lot of help to write this book. Thank you, to the people who went above and beyond or simply inspired me: Marty Jones, Ed Sealover, Kevin Delange, Corey Marshall, the kind staff at the Denver Public Library, Dave Thomas, Tom Noel, Patty Calhoun, Sam Bock, Jason Hanson, Tim Myers, Carl Rose and Dustin Hall. And cheers to everyone who agreed to sit for an interview or drink a beer with me.

I'd like to thank my amazing wife, Sarah, for her patience and support; my parents for everything they've given me; and my kids for putting up with me.

I

FUTURE PAST

From the patio of the new Tivoli Brewing Company in Denver, Corey Marshall can look east toward downtown and up at the twenty-third story of the former MillerCoors building at 1225 East Seventeenth Avenue, where he worked until 2012 as an executive, helping the Golden, Colorado–based beer giant plan strategy, sales tactics and mergers and acquisitions. It had been a good job—one that paid him a nice salary and helped him support his family. But it was missing something.

Back then, Marshall would gaze out of the floor-to-ceiling windows in the other direction—west and down at the Tivoli building, an arresting, Bavarian-style red-brick castle that serves as a student union, offices, meeting and classroom space and a food court for three urban colleges that share the 150-acre Auraria campus.

Marshall had spent a lot of time in that old building—it was painted blue and white for many decades—thirty years earlier when it had also been the home of two legendary 1980s and '90s bars, the Tijuana Yacht Club, where Marshall had been a bouncer while he was in college, and the Boiler Room, where his brother had been a bartender. Marshall had seen the massive, 250-barrel copper brewing kettles that were never removed from the building, ancient brewing equipment that still sat in dark rooms and the smokestack. He'd seen the old signs touting the original, but long-closed, Tivoli Brewing and its beer.

He knew that the building's history went way back. A piece of it was first constructed by brewer Moritz Sigi, a German immigrant who founded Colorado Brewery in 1864. But the additions that gave Tivoli its distinctive look were created between 1880 and 1890 by two other beer men, Max Melsheimer, a Prussian immigrant who ran it as the Milwaukee Brewing Company, and then powerful Denver businessman and German immigrant John Good, who took over in 1900 and changed the name to Tivoli in honor of the world-famous gardens in Copenhagen, Denmark. The Good family continued to grow the brewery for decades. At one point in the 1950s, it was one of the largest breweries west of the Mississippi River, producing 150,000 barrels per year.

But when Good's daughter-in-law Loraine died in 1965, the brewery was sold to brothers Carl and Joseph Occhiato of Pueblo. The Occhiatos introduced a new beer and made plans to expand, but fate wasn't on their side. In 1965, a massive flood along the South Platte River devastated Denver and caused significant damage at Tivoli. A union strike and statewide boycott the next year crippled the business again, and by 1969, it had gone out of business. Though the Tivoli building sat vacant for years after that—the purview of urban explorers and the homeless—and was at one point slated for demolition, it was saved in 1973 after being placed on the National Register of Historic Places.

Around the same time, the Denver Urban Renewal Authority bought the dilapidated building and after several false starts gave it over to the Auraria Higher Education Center, which was just forming. Eventually, the entire complex was renovated and is now the Student Center on the Auraria campus. And through all of that time, its history remained locked inside.

Corey Marshall would find the key to unlock it.

A Denver-area native, Marshall grew up in a middle-class family that had called the city home for three generations. His grandfather used to begin every morning with a Tivoli beer and two raw eggs with salt on top, and when he'd tell stories about Denver in the old days, he always had a Tivoli beer in his hand. He was a Tivoli man until the day he died. In fact, the beers made in that building had been his family's libation of choice dating all the way back to 1912.

Looking down on the grand old building from the Coors offices, Marshall wondered what had become of the company and its employees, recipes and brands. He decided to find out. Armed with a library card and a fierce curiosity, Marshall read dozens of old articles about Tivoli and its predecessors and spinoffs—companies like Rocky Mountain Brewery, Zang's and the Milwaukee Brewery. Then, still out of curiosity, he searched the U.S. Patent and Trademark Office's registry to see if anyone still owned those beer names and brands.

Tivoli Brewing continued to make beer in Denver until 1969. *Library of Congress.*

The old Tivoli Brewing building is now home to the new Tivoli Brewing, founded in 2012. *Corey Marshall.*

No one did. All of them had expired or been abandoned.

What Marshall did next was roll up Denver's entire 160-year brewing history into a single idea, combining his experience at Coors and generations of knowledge and spinning it forward into the modern craft brewing revolution that had bubbled up over the previous decade. It was a way to honor and preserve history and push it forward at the same time.

The year was 2011, and people were beginning to take a new interest in microbreweries, which had weathered a couple of boom and bust cycles since the late 1980s. A handful of new taprooms, including Strange Craft, Caution Brewing, Wit's End, Renegade and Copper Kettle had opened in Denver in the past year, serving everything from classic stouts and IPAs to lagers like pilsners and helle to Belgian-inspired wonders like saisons, tripels and quadrupels. It was the beginning of a stunning new wave of craft brewery openings in the United States that would see the number of beermakers grow from 1,511 in 2007 to more than 8,000 by the end of 2019.

Until then, Marshall had always been a corporate man. After graduating from Colorado State University, he got a job at Ford Motor Company's Denver regional office and was later promoted to roles in Detroit. Marshall paid his way through graduate school at Regis University and then at the University of Detroit. Over the years, he started a family and worked his way up at Ford. But in 1995, his father was diagnosed with Parkinson's disease. It was a devastating moment for Marshall, who had watched his father, an aerospace engineer, build his career, saving money for retirement only to have that retirement taken away by Parkinson's. The Marshalls decided to move home to Colorado.

Before doing so, he researched the best companies to work for in Colorado. Coors was high on the list. In 1996, he began work in Golden, where he focused on capital planning and project construction at the beermaker's many facilities and breweries. But Marshall moved up quickly as Coors grew from a regional powerhouse into a nationwide company, and he learned about every aspect of the brewing business. He also took on leadership roles in sales forecasting, production planning, sales and revenue management, and he bore witness to the infamous pricing wars between the country's big brewers. When Coors merged with Molson in 2005, he moved into offices in a Denver skyscraper on Seventeenth Avenue along with the rest of the company executives. There, he helped manage the post-merger integration and strategy.

As Marshall approached his forty-fifth birthday, though, he began to think about his father more and realized how short life can be. "Reality comes to

Corey Marshall, who re-founded Tivoli Brewing in 2012, during construction. *Corey Marshall.*

you. In the end it's about enjoying what you do. If you have passions, things you want to do, then go do them," he says. That's where Tivoli fit in.

In 2011 and 2012, Marshall began acquiring the trademark rights to dozens of old Colorado brewery names and brands and developing recipes based on those beers. Most of the original recipes had been lost to time or the flood. And even if they hadn't, barley and hops and yeast had changed and evolved to a point where the original ingredients were no longer available and may not have lived up to today's quality standards anyway. So, Marshall got help from Bill Eye, a local lager expert who was then working at Prost Brewing in Denver. Together they re-created the recipe for Tivoli Helles as best as they could.

In 2012, Marshall quit his job at Coors and brewed his first batch of Helles at Prost.

Sales were fine, but Marshall's real goal was to open his own brewery and taproom—and not just anywhere. He wanted the old home of the Tivoli brewery. In 2013, he began negotiating with the Auraria Higher Education Center, and in 2014—in what may have been the most perfect confluence between old and new Denver—he signed a deal to create a brewery, taproom and restaurant in and around the rooms where the original brewery had been.

History doubled back on itself, folding the past into the present.

The university helped pay for renovations, giving Marshall twelve thousand square feet for his brewery (he leased some of that space to a restaurateur to run the kitchen). In return, Metropolitan State University of Denver's hospitality, tourism and events program got to use the brewery to train students in its nascent beer industry program.

In 2017 and 2018, the school renovated three classroom/lab spaces in the basement of the Tivoli, where students now learn about microbiology, production and quality and assurance.

The brewery itself made dozens of reimagined versions of historic Denver lagers, including Neef Brothers Bohemian Girl Pilsner from 1891; Sigi's Wild Horse Bock Beer, dating to the 1860s; Hi En Brau Swiss Dunkel from the 1950s; and Tivoli Jet Malt Liquor from the 1960s. But it also pushed forward, developing recipes for modern styles like a Strawberry Mint Berliner Weiss, a Hoppy Marzen Lager, an altbier, pale ales, IPAs and double IPAs.

Marshall continued to research the history of Denver's breweries and gather artifacts, stories and interviews from the people who were involved with the Tivoli over the decades. He has also traveled to Europe to learn more about the brewing traditions of some of the first immigrant brewers who came to Denver in the 1850s and 1860s.

By 2018, Metro State, with Tivoli's help, was offering two bachelor of science degrees in beer: brewery operations and craft brewing and pub operations. It also offers a brewing minor and certificate. The teaching staff come from a variety of backgrounds, including brewing and science, while the guidance committee and guest lecturers are made up of employees of

Tivoli workers hamming it up in the early part of the twentieth century. *Corey Marshall.*

some of Colorado's most well-known breweries, along with other brewing industry professionals.

And finally, in 2018, Tivoli opened a second location inside the Westin hotel that adjoins the Denver International Airport. Students work there as well, brewing beer for the airport.

Marshall stepped away from day-to-day operations at Tivoli that same year, leaving it with new investors, who moved the packaging away from its historic look and toward a trendier feel—but kept the storied legacy as part of its marketing.

It was a big change, but then again, the Tivoli has undergone a lot of changes. In a historic account of the Tivoli, the authors of "Bavaria of the Rockies," which was published in pamphlet form in 1985, quote Tivoli general manager Howard Hosek, who in 1969, was optimistic that the Tivoli would be able to rebound from the double disasters it faced in 1965 and 1966, not to mention the competition it faced. Though the company closed shortly after Hosek made his comments, one of them turned out to more prescient that even he could have known.

"I think there is still a place in Denver for the Tivoli," he said.

2

FIRST BEERS

When Frederick Zadek Salomon pulled his wagon up to the confluence of the South Platte River and Cherry Creek on June 20, 1859, he gazed out over a muddy mess.

Slow, brown and a half a mile wide in some places, the Platte jumped its banks each spring when the snow melted in the Rocky Mountains and shriveled up into a thick, shallow sludge in summer. Arapaho and Cheyenne camps dotted the banks in some places, along with cottonwood groves and a couple of lively, if ramshackle, mining camps.

A year earlier, a gold-hunting party that was camped at the confluence found what they were looking for in a stream a few miles away. It wasn't the first report of gold in the South Platte and its tributaries, but it was the largest, and it sparked a wave of speculators who began to pour in from all directions. The Pikes Peak Gold Rush, as it was known—despite the fact that Pikes Peak was some eighty-five miles to the south—would eventually bring more than 100,000 people to what was then called the Kansas Territory.

Although many of those fortune-seekers quickly turned around and headed home when they couldn't find gold in the river right away, others pushed farther into the mountains where the real riches were, creating camps that would become towns like Idaho Springs, Georgetown, Black Hawk, Central City, Como, South Park and Fairplay.

These Fifty-Niners also built a handful of towns around the confluence of the South Platte and Cherry Creek to serve and supply the miners. These towns included Auraria on the south side of the confluence, where the

Auraria campus is now, and Denver City on the east side, where Larimer Square now sits alongside Union Station and LoDo. Denver absorbed Auraria in April 1860.

Salomon, a twenty-nine-year-old Jewish Prussian immigrant, operated a general store in New Mexico before heeding the call of the gold rush. His plan was to set up a similar operation in Auraria. By fall, Salomon, his two brothers and various business partners had constructed a one-story wooden building and acquired a couple of others, including one at the corner of Tenth and Saint Louis Streets (now Tenth and Larimer Streets) roughly where the Auraria Events Center now stands on the Auraria campus. There, he and fellow immigrant Charles Tascher fired up their kettles and formed the Rocky Mountain Brewery.

Denver's first batch of beer was brewed on November 10, 1859, and was ready to drink by December 6. That's when Tascher delivered a bottle to the *Rocky Mountain News*, which was founded in April of the same year and was one of the region's first newspapers. The beer probably didn't taste very good

ROCKY MOUNTAIN BREWERY
Brewery Block, Highland.
Solomon Endlich & Good, Proprietors

A drawing of Denver's first brewery, Rocky Mountain Brewery, founded in 1859. *J.E. Dillingham, Artist, W.H. Rease & Co., lithographer, History Colorado.*

by today's standards—early on, Salomon and Tascher didn't have access to a reliable source of malt, and they had little, if any, hops. But to the locals, it was heaven compared to the strychnine whiskey and Taos Lightning they were used to drinking.

And any beer is good beer when it's free. Salomon and Tascher delivered a full keg of free beer to the paper a few weeks later, prompting *Rocky Mountain News* editor William Byers to write that it was "the best we ever tasted." Thus began a long and noble tradition in which breweries have plied the media with their wares—a tradition that happily continues today.

Sales were apparently strong enough that in January 1860, the partners began construction of a larger production plant across the South Platte at Seventh and Water Streets, where the Denver Aquarium and its parking lots are today. But supplies in this frontier town must have continued to be a problem because the brewery had to assure readers in a June 1860 ad in the *Rocky Mountain News* that "they have received their Spring Stock of Barley, Malt and Hops, and will now keep constantly on hand a good supply of Lager Beer and Ale, at their Brewery."

That steady supply of hops may have been thanks to another entrepreneur named John Good. Like Salomon and Tascher, Good, then twenty-four, was also an immigrant, having left his home in Ahrweiler, in what is now Germany, in 1857. After spending time in Ohio, he arrived in Denver a month before Salomon and established his own mercantile shop.

One oft-repeated story has it that Good—who would later become a towering figure in Denver's nascent brewing industry—crossed the plains alone and rode into Denver on a wagon full of hops like a beer-soaked Lone Ranger, but there is no record of that happening. A more likely version of the story is that Salomon made a trip to St. Louis after starting the brewery, gathering imported hops, midwestern barley and a lager yeast strain.

Whatever the truth, Good quickly established himself as a successful merchant and financier, and by the spring of 1860, he had teamed up with Salomon and another immigrant named Charles Endlich to buy out Tascher's share of the Rocky Mountain Brewery. The three men continued building the new brewing facility on Water Street, and it was finished that August. It included a gravity brewing system, a steam engine and boiler, an ice cellar, a stable with horses, a beer wagon and hundreds of wooden kegs and barrels of different sizes.

In 1861, Endlich and Good bought out Salomon, who went on to find his fortune in other industries. Endlich then bought out Good, but when

Endlich died in 1864, Good, repurchased the brewery, and in 1871, he sold it to another immigrant named Philip Zang.

This kind of partnering was normal for the German-speaking immigrants of the time, many of whom teamed up to start hotels, stores and banks, as well as water and utility companies. In fact, Salomon and Good were part of a wave of thousands of Europeans who crossed the ocean to seek their fortunes. Many left areas that are now Germany, Austria, Poland, the Czech Republic and other countries in the late 1840s and 1850s amid political unrest and violence that began in 1848. Some were part of a movement, called the Forty-Eighters, who sought a more democratic government and improvements in human rights and working conditions. These rebellions were mostly quashed, though, leaving their proponents with no choice but to leave or face possible retribution. Now these Forty-Eighters were Fifty-Niners.

For the brewers among these immigrants, the timing was right. A new type of beer called lager had just been introduced to the United States a decade earlier. Lagers are made with a strain of yeast that works more slowly and at colder temperatures than ales (lager yeast also ferments at the bottom of a brewing tank rather than at the top). It typically produces liquid that is lighter in color and mouthfeel and lower in alcohol. It also has a cleaner taste. Style examples include pilsner, helles and bock. Most people credit a Bavarian brewer named John Wagner with bringing the first lager yeast to the United States in 1840, when he sailed on a clipper ship to Philadelphia. Though the Germans had been brewing with lager yeast for a long time, previous attempts to introduce it to the United States may have failed because the older ships were slower and the yeast would no longer be viable once it arrived.

Lager was immediately popular with German- and Polish-speaking immigrants since that's what they were used to. But it also caught on with those who were born in the States. English-style ales, which had dominated the New World since the 1600s, were dark, bitter and often murky, which could make them unappetizing. Lagers, on the other hand, were brighter and sparklier and looked beautiful in a glass—the vessel that was replacing leather, pewter or ceramic mugs, says Carl Rose, a former brewer at Longmont's Left Hand Brewing and a historian who wrote his master's thesis on pre-Prohibition beermakers in Colorado. "Just like today, an easy-to-drink lager appeals to a wider population and flavor palate."

By the 1850s, lager had started to take off, and by the 1870s, the lovely golden liquid was "outselling ale hand over fist," Rose says. "There was an immigrant boom that was used to drinking lagers, so there was demand for lager breweries. Eventually, this immigrant boom moved west and took advantage of the opportunities."

Salomon, Tascher, Good and Endlich must have had access to lager yeast as well because, although they also brewed ales like porters and cream ales, they specialized in lager.

So did the breweries that followed.

In 1864, Moritz Sigi, originally of Baden, Germany, founded the Colorado Brewery close to where Salomon and Tascher had built their first enterprise, at Tenth and Larimer Streets. Sigi, who had tried his hand at prospecting and baking, found success quickly, especially after lubing up the editors at the *Rocky Mountain News*, who described his beer as "second to none."

Four years later, in 1868, Sigi constructed a building next to his Colorado Brewery called Sigi's Hall, which acted as a meeting place and clubhouse for German-speaking immigrants. He also expanded the brewery, which specialized in buck beer, adding a barley malting kiln to his grain mill, brew kettles, an icehouse and storage rooms. These buildings formed the foundation of what is now the Tivoli Student Union on the Auraria campus.

Denver was growing quickly as well. Real buildings replaced lean-tos. Streets replaced wagon trails, and governments replaced frontier justice. There was still no electricity and no major railroad connection, but there were plenty of speculators, fortune-seekers, hustlers, merchants and miners.

All of them needed a drink, and they'd find plenty.

3
BREWERY BOOMTOWN

In 1869, John Good, who had reacquired Rocky Mountain Brewery after Charles Endlich's death, hired an enterprising Bavarian brewer named Philip Zang to take charge of the operation. By this time, the brewery was producing about two thousand barrels per year. Zang had learned his trade in Germany before coming to the United States in 1853 and opening the Phoenix Brewery in Louisville, Kentucky. Zang did well, and in 1871, he bought the brewery from Good.

Energetic and well-connected, Zang grew the operation quickly, distributing beer throughout Colorado, from the mining towns to farm and ranch country. But manufacturing plants were dangerous places in those days, and tragedy struck in 1875 when the brewery caught fire and burned to the ground. Zang rebuilt but was hit with yet another fire in 1881.

Undaunted, Zang and his son, Adolph, rebuilt once again—this time creating a massive brick-and-stone complex that included a huge brewhouse, lager tanks, a malting kiln, an icehouse, a cooperage for making barrels, stables for the horses and carts that delivered his beer. They also built a family home, hotel and boardinghouse for employees and railroad spurs that connected the brewery to the main rail line, which had finally come through town in 1870. Now known as Philip Zang and Company, the brewery invested in modern equipment, including newer, smaller boilers and mechanical refrigeration, which allowed lager breweries to produce year-round (lager needs to ferment at colder temperatures than ale, which is why, historically, it could only be made in certain regions and during certain times of the year).

"Zang was very forward-looking," says historian Carl Rose. "Back then, if you didn't have money to buy a refrigeration machine so you could make ice and brew year-round, you were at a disadvantage. Smaller breweries that didn't have access to capital couldn't compete." In addition to new technology, Zang also incorporated scientific advancements like pasteurization.

A decade earlier, when Fred Salomon first built Rocky Mountain Brewery on the other side of the South Platte, he probably used horses to generate the power needed to run hot water and grain through rudimentary pumps. "They were brewing the same way that they had been doing it for hundreds of years," Rose says, including the use of gravity brewing systems.

By the time Zang and Company was at its height, the brewery was efficiently turning out 110,000 to 150,000 barrels of beer per year and was the largest brewery between St. Louis and San Francisco. Its brands included Pilsener, High Grade, Silver State and Columbine. Like other breweries, most of it was shipped in wooden barrels, although Zang was one of the first to heavily invest in bottled beer, so he could send it in small quantities to Colorado's mining towns, where it could compete with the small breweries that sprang up in those places.

The Zang brewery in its heyday in the 1890s. *William Henry Jackson Collection, History Colorado.*

In 1880, there were 2,266 breweries in the United States. It was a booming industry that attracted foreign investors, especially those in the United Kingdom. A wave of British investment followed, and it's estimated that some twenty-four British business syndicates spent $90 million to buy around 80 U.S. breweries. They would often buy multiple breweries in one city, such as St. Louis, New Orleans or New York, and merge them.

Zang, now a millionaire, sold his brewery to one of these groups, the City of London Contract Corporation, which had already purchased breweries in more than a dozen U.S. cities. This particular syndicate bought two other breweries for $2.5 million.

Denver United Breweries Limited, as the combined operation was called, wielded a lot of power in the market this way. It could afford to lower prices to hurt competitors or control access to the consumers by purchasing more saloons. Rose sees some parallels to the tactics that large breweries use today when it comes to buying or competing with small craft breweries.

Philip Zang continued to run the plant until 1892, when he retired and turned the management over to his son, Adolph. But the role was an honorary one, and Adolph himself was more focused on other business interests, including banking, hotels, mining, horses, real estate and even the development of Lakeside Amusement Park.

By that time, many other breweries had come and gone in Denver. They included One Horse Brewery, which operated briefly in 1864 around Seventeenth and Blake Streets; Parkhurst's Brewery, which opened on Larimer Street in 1870 and was later known as Eastern Brewery; Davidson Brewery, which opened in 1870 around what is now Seventeenth and Wazee Streets; Villa Park, located in west Denver in 1872; Block and Rusch Weis Brewery, founded in 1875 and located on Lawrence and Eighteenth Streets; and Lion Brewing and Bottling, which ran a brewery and bottling plant at Eighth and Larimer starting in 1879.

A larger brewery was City Brewery, founded in 1871, in what is now the Lower Highland neighborhood of Denver. It later became Union Brewing in 1892 and then merged with Tivoli a decade later to form the Tivoli-Union Brewing Company. Another was the Denver Ale Company, founded in 1869 by a couple of Chicagoans to improve the quality of porters and cream ales in Denver. It began producing lagers at the corner of Ninth and Mariposa Streets in 1871 when it was taken over by a different team of men who changed the name to Denver Brewing Company. The group eventually sold, like Zang, to the City of London Contract Corporation.

There were also a variety of short-lived brewery/bar combinations, such as the Springer Saloon and Brewery on a notorious stretch of Holladay Street, which was also home to Denver's red-light district. Now called Market Street, it was renamed because the Holladay family didn't like the association with drunkenness and prostitution.

Moritz Sigi, meanwhile, had become a city councilman and a successful businessman with his Colorado Brewery. Sadly, he was killed in 1874, when his family's buggy overturned after the horses were startled. The brewery continued to run for some time but was put up for auction and purchased in 1879 by Max Melsheimer, a Prussian immigrant who had been brewing in Milwaukee for nine years before moving to Denver.

Melsheimer borrowed $250,000 from none other than John Good to upgrade the brewery, greatly increasing capacity and renaming it Milwaukee Brewery. But Melsheimer was in over his head by 1882, which is when Good foreclosed on his loan and took over the brewery. He renamed it Tivoli and oversaw the construction and expansion that gave the building the distinctive grandeur it exudes today. After that, Tivoli would stay in the Good family for many decades, becoming one of the West's largest breweries and a Denver staple.

The last major brewery to hold sway in Denver before the turn of the twentieth century was Western Brewing/Neef Brothers Brewing. Founded in 1890 by John P. Dostal, it was acquired the next year by brothers Frederick and Maximilian Neef, who had come to the United States from a town close to where John Good was born in what is now Germany.

The brothers had gotten their start in Denver twenty years earlier when they opened a saloon called Neef's Hall. Shortly thereafter, though, they went into the wholesale business, distributing liquor throughout Colorado. They also operated a bar that eventually became the Buckhorn Exchange, which is still going strong today.

Located at what is now Twelfth Avenue and Quivas Street, the five-story Neef Brothers brewery was expanded several times as the company grew. Though it faced stiff competition from Zang and Coors, Neef Brothers managed to thrive until Prohibition. Its lager beers included Gold Belt, Bohemia Girl Special Brew and Wiener Maerzen.

Today's craft brewers often tout their local connections, working to use Colorado-grown hops, barley and other ingredients and supplies. But this tradition goes back more than one hundred years. Both Zang and the Neef brothers frequently bragged about buying Colorado malt, coal and other products. In fact, Philip Zang is often credited for creating the barley business

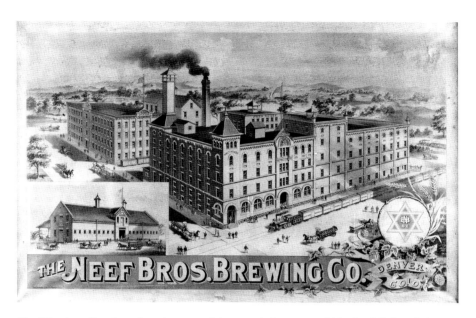

Neef Brothers Brewing, circa the turn of the twentieth century. *Richard and Kathryn Ralston Colorado Advertising Collection, History Colorado.*

in the state. He was also quoted in newspapers as saying that people should buy his beer rather than that of Anheuser-Busch because the money stayed in the community. That refrain is familiar to craft beer drinkers today, who often hear the same from local breweries.

Of course, Zang eventually sold out to Denver United Breweries, the English syndicate, a fact that isn't lost on Rose. "There is a lesson there for the craft brewers of today," he says.

4
ROCKY MOUNTAIN SPRING WATER

If he could do it over, Pete Coors would have insisted that his brewery's headquarters stay in Colorado after the company merged with SAB Miller in 2008. "I'm probably going to get into trouble for saying this, but one of biggest mistakes we made was moving it to Chicago," he said in a 2018 interview. "We lost the connection to the brewery. Knowing the beer, being able to smell it and taste it in this environment. It's important." (His comments took on a sharper note in late 2019 when Molson Coors announced that it would close its Denver offices entirely and lay off more than three hundred people.)

It was a surprising thing for a corporate executive to say but not all that surprising for a member of the Coors family, and it helps explain why the company took such an unusual path to becoming one of the biggest brewing companies in the world.

"It's an older brewery and it has its challenges, but it's deep into the DNA of what makes us Coors," Pete's son, Peter J. Coors, who has held several management roles with the company, said during that same 2018 interview. "The Golden Brewery is on the same piece of land that we started on 1873. None of the original buildings are still around, but with the land, with the Rocky Mountain water, that's what made the Coors brand."

Coors, after all, has always been in Colorado—since before there even was a Colorado. Founded in 1873 by Adolph Herman Joseph Coors, the brewery was up and running three years before Colorado was incorporated as the thirty-eighth state in the Union.

Adolph Herman Joseph Coors Sr. founded Coors Brewing in 1873. *Coors Brewing.*

Adolph had come looking for that good spring water.

Born in 1847 in Barmen, Germany (then part of Prussia), Adolph learned several trades as a teenager and became a brewer's apprentice at the age of fourteen. His parents died the next year, and although he and his siblings went to live in an orphanage, Adolph continued to work at the brewery, learning several sides of the business. But at the age of twenty-one, Adolph decided—like Fred Salomon, John Good and many other brewers before him—to leave Prussia rather than live in a kingdom where he opposed the politics of the time and could be in danger or arrested.

Adolph stowed away on a ship bound for Baltimore. Though he was discovered, he agreed to pay the cost of his passage once he found a job. In America, Adolph, whose original surname had actually been Kuhrs, changed it, learned English and found employment doing menial labor. In 1969, he moved to Illinois to work at the Stenger Brewery. Three years later, he headed west to the Colorado Territory.

He tried his hand at several jobs, all the while looking for a good water source to open his own brewery. He found it near an abandoned tannery along the banks of Clear Creek in Golden, where dozens of springs provided ample fresh water.

While Denver was quickly becoming a real city, other towns were also growing. Golden, then called Golden City, had been founded a year after Denver and was a waystation between the city and the mining towns in the mountains. Situated between two mesas known as North and South Table Mountain, it developed in what people called the "last flat place" before the real hills began. The town was so important, in fact, that it became the capital of the Colorado Territory in 1862.

With financial backing from a German immigrant named Jacob Schueler, Adolph got to work, hiring employees and building the brewery, an icehouse, a malting kiln and a bottling plant. Since Denver already had its share of breweries, Adolph focused on the mining towns, using his proximity to the railroad tracks to ship kegs and bottles of his sole product, Golden Lager Beer, to the taverns and saloons in the hills.

By 1880, the brewery had become hugely successful, and Coors was able to buy out Schueler and expand the company himself. He eventually added two new products, Coors Export Beer and Pilsener Lager Beer and began distributing to other nearby states.

He hired mostly German-speaking immigrants like himself, treating them like family and hosting events and parties in a large, family-friendly beer garden that came complete with a lake for paddle boats. "They were very much about being part of the community," says historian Carl Rose. Adolph knew the names of all of his employees—a practice that he passed down to his children and grandchildren. There was also free beer for his workers—always free beer.

Tight money management helped Coors continue to grow quickly and weather the silver crash of 1893 and fierce competition from other breweries.

And although Adolph eventually built a mansion for his family in Golden, the family didn't spend lavishly.

"My uncle [Bill Coors, who died in 2018 at the age of 102] told us stories about the daughters of the big Denver brewers, like Zang and Tivoli," Pete Coors recalls. "They were always dripping in jewelry and furs, and the poor Coorses in Golden got nothing. But that was his attitude. We put the money back into the business."

But in 1894, an event took place that would change and harden Adolph beyond his already staunch mindset and affect the decisions of future generations.

Well-established and eager to build the business further, Adolph took out a loan for $90,000—a huge amount of money at the time. On Memorial Day of that year, Clear Creek jumped its banks after heavy rain and began flooding the factory and approaching the mansion. Seeing what was happening, Adolph quickly put hundreds of men to work digging a channel and altering the path of the water.

But the flood had done its damage. Not only was Coors unable to pay back the original loan, but he also had to take out a second $90,000 loan with a substantial interest rate to clean up the mess. It reminded Adolph of when he'd been caught onboard the ship to America when he was twenty-one, and he vowed to never borrow another dollar or rely on anyone else for money. He didn't. And neither did his son, Adolph II, or Adolph II's sons, Bill, Joe and Ad.

"We talk a lot about sacred cows and about doing things the right way," explains Pete. "We didn't have any debt until 1996, when we opened our second brewery in [Virginia's] Shenandoah Valley. There was a reason for that. My great-grandfather was very successful. But things change. We are in a different place now."

The flood was a defining moment that helps explain some of the Coors family culture that has both delighted and confounded outsiders for generations. Insular, smart and stubborn, the Coors family's greatest strengths have often been its biggest weaknesses as well, and the history of both the clan and the company are full of apparent contradictions and dichotomies that don't always make sense.

How can a family known for its outspoken right-wing politics and millions of dollars in support of far-right foundations also run a company that is admired for having some of the earliest and most progressive policies toward gay marriage and benefits?

How can the same company that illegally dumped hundreds of thousands of gallons of beer into rivers and pleaded guilty to and paid fines

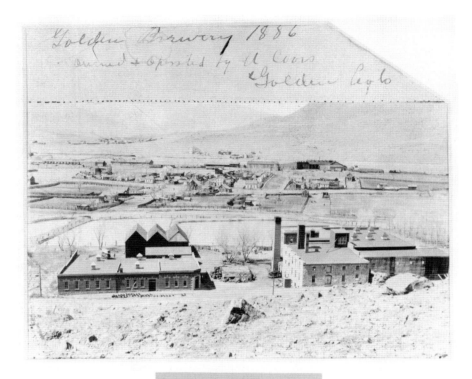

Coors Golden Brewery · 1886

The Coors Brewery in 1886, thirteen years after it opened in Golden. *Coors Brewing.*

for hundreds of broken air, water and toxic waste laws also be regarded as one of the most forward-thinking when it comes to renewable energy and wastewater recycling and gather plaudits for diverting nearly 100 percent of its waste products at several plants from landfills?

Why would a company that went out of its way to make its employees feel like family also force would-be Latino employees to take lie detector tests and fight against unions with staggering vitriol?

The answers start with Adolph, a man who knew the name of every one of his employees but kept his own children at a distance—a patriarchal figure who is still revered by his descendants but whose personality was so big that it still casts a shadow over almost everything the family and the company do today.

But there is more to it than that, Pete says now. Adolph was a firm believer in "the code of the west," where you do things yourself, you do

The Coors Brewing plant in Golden in the 1960s. *Coors Brewing.*

them right and your handshake is your word. He valued personal integrity, fair play and, of course, a high-quality product. That code of ethics still guides the Coors family, and although Pete acknowledges that it got the company "into trouble sometimes," it also helped sustain Coors and keep it alive. "It's something that has been handed down from generation to generation," he says.

Indeed, after the turn of the century, the Coors family fortunes continued to improve, and Adolph's son, Adolph II, who had a similar outlook on the world as his father, took on a larger role at the company starting in 1909. But both men could see that the temperance movement was growing, and around the same time, they began to diversify their business interests, investing in cement and ceramics.

By 1915, the company was second only to the Zang Brewery when it came to beer production, but Prohibition in Colorado—and then nationwide— put an end to that. To maintain itself and to keep its people employed, Coors began making "non-alcoholic cereal beverages," and malted milk, in addition to cement and ceramics. While the near-beer didn't do very well, Coors was able to get by with the malted milk, which it sold to candy companies and ice cream parlors.

In 1929, while Coors was at one of its bleakest points, Adolph—the man who never gave in—paradoxically took his own life at the age of sixty-one, jumping from the sixth story of a hotel in Virginia Beach, Virginia.

Just four years later, Prohibition ended, and Coors was back in business. Adolph II, who had studied at the knee of his father, dedicated himself to moving forward. He hired new employees, invested in technology and began doing research on his own ingredients. At the time, Coors was down to one product, Export Lager, but in 1937, the company added the lighter beer that would become Coors Banquet and began experimenting with the recipes that would become Coors Light in 1978. It also introduced the slogan "Brewed with Pure Rocky Mountain Spring Water," which would become iconic over the next several decades.

Adolph II was known for his six-day-a-week work ethic and his refusal to compromise on quality. "He nurtured Coors from a virtually unknown company producing less than 100,000 barrels of beer in 1933 to a nationally recognized brewery producing more than 7 million barrels per year at the time of his death [in 1970]," writes Russ Banham in *Coors: A Rocky Mountain Legend*. It was also during this time that Coors established its original eleven-state footprint in the West, which would stay the same until the late 1970s, when Coors began a slow expansion across the Mississippi River.

In the 1940s and '50s, Adolph II's three sons, Adolph III (known as Ad), Bill and Joe, began to work their way through the company ranks, toiling in a variety of jobs and furthering their father's goals. Ad eventually became CEO, while his brothers, Bill in particular, oversaw a string of technological advances and expansions.

The most well known of these advances took place in the 1950s and began with the replacement of the beer industry's container of choice at the time: the tin can. Bill, an engineer, didn't like the metallic aftertaste that the tin imparted, and the company was looking for a way to make its beer taste fresher—something the staff thought they could do if they stopped pasteurizing it, which requires heat. (Ironically, the development of pasteurization, which kills bacteria that can grow in beer, is what had helped breweries like Coors, Zang and Tivoli safely ship their products to other states in the previous century.) Bill and his staff eventually created the seamless aluminum beer can after a lot of time, energy and expense. It caused a stir in the industry but eventually became the standard.

Not only did the can get rid of the aftertaste, but it also allowed the brewery to stop pasteurizing the beer because aluminum cans could be filled in a more sterile way. The fresher taste of the beer became one of the brewery's calling cards. Coors was also suffering an image problem due to the tin cans that littered the sides of roadways, streams and anywhere else people threw them. So, once the company switched to aluminum, Bill began to investigate the idea of recycling. That effort was successful as well, and Coors later became the first brewery to pay customers to bring back cans.

When Coors stopped pasteurizing its beer, it came up with the then-novel approach of keeping the beer cold from the plant to the store, introducing refrigerated rail cars and trucks and asking its distributors to build refrigerated warehouses. The move shook the industry once again and scored another marketing victory.

This long period of prosperity was punctured by a dark chapter in the Coors family history, though—one that would have as much impact on the family psyche as the flood of 1894. In 1960, Ad, the forty-four-year-old CEO, was killed during a botched kidnapping attempt as he drove to work. Since the family received a ransom note, they didn't know what had happened for months, and the saga played out in the papers on a daily basis and inspired the biggest manhunt in U.S. history up to that point.

In 1961, the drama came to an end when the kidnapper was caught and Ad's body was discovered, but it obviously took a heavy toll on the Coors family members, who hardened their hearts to the outside world and became even more insular than in the past.

Still, the company continued to grow. Adolph II passed away, but the mantle was picked up by Bill and Joe, who continued to innovate. Coors went public in 1975 and became the fifth-largest brewery in the nation by 1977, even as distribution stayed limited. That same year, though, Coors and the main union representing its employees began a disruptive, angry war that would last ten years. On one side were boycotts, pickets and national headlines. On the other was a family that felt betrayed by its employees, many of whom had worked at Coors for decades. Coors took a hard line against the union, and it eventually won, though the battle left a lot of scars.

While there was anger in Colorado, the rest of the country seemed to love Coors more than ever, clamoring for the beer made with Rocky Mountain Spring Water. The television commercials helped, as did *Smokey and the Bandit*, which was released in 1977. By the mid-1980s, Coors was a household name; the brewery had finally crossed the Mississippi River in 1981, and its products were sold in all fifty states by 1991.

Pete Coors, who had started working summers in the family firm in the late '60s while he was still in college, grew up with a similar mentality to his father, Joe, and his uncle Bill, but the world was changing, and Pete had to change along with it. He says, "When I started working during the summers in college, I knew everybody. But now we have 18,000 employees. It's difficult because you can't know everybody. That piece of the company just doesn't exist anymore."

Coors was now a billion-dollar corporation with shareholders, power, political clout and bankers—yes, bankers. By the time Pete became vice-chairman and CEO of the company in 1993, Coors had borrowed money again and would continue to do so to finance additional brewing facilities in other states.

At home, the company was helping to bring the Colorado Rockies to Denver, creating Blue Moon and establishing its name on Coors Field. But across the country, Coors was heavily engaged in pricing and advertising wars with the makers of Miller and Bud. Television ads featuring waterfalls and cowboys had given way to the infamous "and twins" ad, and the Silver Bullet (Coors Light) ruled the airwaves.

The late '80s and early '90s were also the beginnings of the craft beer explosion—something that Coors is often credited with helping to encourage. In fact, Dave Thomas, who worked for Coors for thirty-two years, says that once Bill Coors got wind of the microbreweries in the late '80s, he told his brewing team that if they ever got a call for help with technical assistance from a microbrewer, they should "get on an airplane and go. He said, 'Don't worry about competition. We will compete with them on the shelf.'"

Part of the reason for his altruism had to do with business, of course. History was never far from the minds of the Coors family, and Prohibition seemed like it was only yesterday. They never knew when it might rear its ugly head again. "He said, 'These people will provide the kind of credibility in Washington, D.C. that we can't buy as big companies,'" Thomas remembers. And he was right. Microbrewers added more voices to any debate about beer.

Thomas, who was the director of brewing research and development for ten years before ending his service with Coors in 2007 as a traveling brewmaster, now works part-time as a brewer for Dostal Alley, a Central City casino and brewery. He is also a consultant, a board member for the Craft Maltsters Guild and the author of *Of Mines and Beer*, a seminal history of Colorado's mountain-town breweries.

Pete Coors highlighted
Rocky Mountain Spring
water in numerous television
commercials. *Coors Brewing.*

At Coors, he had the chance to help dozens of microbreweries around the country, like Boulder Beer Company and Snake River Brewing in Idaho. "We would sell them bottles or malt, and we would work with them on their labs and tell them how to set things up," he says. "Never say 'no' to anyone: that was a direct order from Bill."

Pete Coors says sharing knowledge was good for the entire industry and that it followed along with his family's ethos of being helpful—just as Coors is reputed to have pumped out Tivoli Brewing's basement when it flooded in 1965—of being good citizens and competing fair and square. It's also part of the reason why he gets frustrated by some craft brewers these days, especially the Boulder-based Brewers Association trade group, which has waged a war of words with Coors over issues like independence and truth in labeling. "They like to poke us in the eye, which is kind of annoying, like mosquitos," he says. "But there is a lot more animosity coming toward us from them than we have going out."

Of course, it's easy to avoid animosity when you are a $4.3 billion multinational making 33 million barrels of beer per year, which Coors was at the end of 2004, just before it merged with Canada's Molson Brewing. Then, two years later, the combined company formed a joint venture with SAB Miller, bringing former competitors together so they could team up against Anheuser-Busch, which would be acquired by InBev, the world's largest brewery, in 2008.

MillerCoors put its headquarters in Chicago, a neutral location, but Coors kept its downtown Denver offices at 1225 Seventeenth Street, where Corey Marshall worked and would look out at the Tivoli building. In 2014, the company moved a few blocks over, to 1801 California Street, where it occupied the forty-fifth, forty-sixth and forty-seventh floors until the end of 2019.

In 2016, AB InBev struck a deal to buy SAB Miller, ending its partnership with Coors. As part of the purchase, however, AB InBev was forced to spin off its holdings in Miller, which it sold to Coors. Then, in late 2019, Molson Coors announced that it would shutter its Denver offices altogether, a move that shocked Colorado. It was also announced that Pete would retire from his day-to-day job there.

With every one of these changes, the Coors family lost a little bit more of Adolph's company as outside executive and directors gained power. But it did not lose all of it. Although the family owns less than 15 percent of the company now, it still wields some clout. Pete's sons, Peter and David, are both executives now, although neither one is sure to move up the ladder. "It's an added burden when your name is Coors," Pete said. "And you don't just start at the top. There is too much at stake these days. You don't want anyone to fail, but you really don't want a member of the family to fail, so they have to be just as smart as the people we hire."

Among the Coors family members, Peter has risen the furthest. An engineer with a degree from Cornell University, like his father, grandfather and great-uncle before him, Peter has served in several executive roles.

But like the other men in the Coors family, he also tries to keep his hands on the pulse of what has always made Coors the company it is. "I like to go to the brewery and talk to people," he says. "And I like to go to bars and ask people whether they like the beer and why. We can do focus groups and all the research we want, but the bar is where you find out what's really going on."

5

FROM WET TO DRY

Booze and gambling. Gambling and booze. Brothels, brawls and bedlam. To believe many old accounts of Denver in the 1890s, the ever-growing boomtown was more like Sodom and Gomorrah than St. Louis and Chicago. Saloons lined the sides of Blake and Market Streets, where a train depot had finally replaced the old stage stop in the 1870s. From there, they spilled out into the surrounding blocks like Larimer, Lawrence and Curtis Streets.

Prostitution was rampant, it seems, and violence was everywhere. Men were drinking at work and on their lunch breaks or ignoring work altogether in favor of the tavern. They'd pay children or down-on-their-luck types to head to the saloons and bring them tin pails—often lined with lard to prevent leaking—full of beer, a seamy practice known as "rushing the growler" (which is where the modern-day term for the to-go vessels comes from). On-the-job mayhem, accidents, explosions and disasters were commonplace. When the drinking got boring by itself, the men began fighting in the streets, firing their pistols or their rifles in the air and beating their wives and kids.

"For drinking sprees, whoring, crime, business and labor meetings, and other activities, Denverites, other Coloradans, and visitors resorted to the Queen City's numerous bars," writes preeminent Denver historian and professor Tom Noel in *The City and Saloon: Denver 1858–1916*. "Denver became a binge town, a city where bars catered to visitors from surrounding mines, ranches, railroads, military bases and farms."

In the city's early years, in the 1860s and '70s, saloons, pubs and taverns had served as offices, meeting places, post offices, ad hoc banks, doctor's quarters, community centers and even churches. German and Irish immigrants were accustomed to this kind of culture, which often included family activities, so they mimicked the traditions of their homelands when they came to Denver.

But things changed as the city grew and gained a reputation for the Wild West. "At the turn of century, there was a shift toward public drinking and overindulgence. Women were no longer welcome, and drinking in public for them became taboo," historian Carl Rose explains (women were actually banned from saloons by a Denver judge in 1901). Taverns and saloons became a breeding ground for alcoholism, poverty, sickness and crime. They were also great places to get rich, and the city's breweries wasted no time preying on working-class grunts who toiled in smelters, mines, cattle yards and the other industrial shops that had sprung up around the railroads over the previous two decades.

Bar-room custom and etiquette at the time called for men to "treat" one another to drinks when they had the money. Once someone was treated to a beer, however, he'd feel obligated to reciprocate until eventually the rounds were flying around the saloon, one after another. "It was seen as the gentlemanly thing to do," Rose says. "So if there were four guys in the bar, eventually they'd each end up drinking four beers instead of one or two."

Brewery employees, aware of this custom, would often deliver treating money to saloon owners along with their kegs and encourage them to kick things off in hopes of selling more beer. It was a smart strategy that resulted in higher sales and much more drunkenness. Furthermore, since the saloons didn't have any kind of legal or cultural liability for their customers, "they would serve them beer until they passed out, push them out the door and then wake them up in the morning and serve them more beer," Rose says.

By the late 1890s, there had been significant consolidation among the breweries, and only a handful of players had any real market share in Denver. These included Tivoli, Union Brewing, Neef Brothers and Coors. Zang's and Denver Brewing, both owned by the English conglomerate, also controlled a huge part of the business. (Another dozen or so breweries operated across the state in Central City, Trinidad, Pueblo, Leadville and Silverton, among others.) Out-of-state breweries like Anheuser-Busch, Schlitz, Pabst and Blatz, made inroads into Colorado thanks to the railroads, the discovery of pasteurization and the modern bottle cap, known as a crown cap, which replaced corks. And it was all-out war between these players.

L.G. Renhard's Saloon in the Globeville neighborhood boasted its affiliation with Coors, circa 1901. *The Stephen H. Hart Library and Research Center/History Colorado.*

Since there were few regulations in place, the big breweries not only made the beer, but they also sold and distributed it by carriage or by train. They also began buying up saloons where they could serve their products exclusively. But that wasn't all. "Breweries bought saloons or arranged mortgages, loans and other financial commitments that would tie saloonkeepers to their products," Tom Noel writes. "If the saloonkeepers defaulted on their loans, the breweries would take over the business." If the saloonkeepers continued to serve multiple brands of beers, the breweries would use a variety of strongarm techniques, intimidation and even violence to convince them to do otherwise.

While the breweries battled one another, however, there were bigger forces at work that were targeting everyone in the liquor industry and the alcoholic culture.

The temperance movement wasn't new at the turn of the nineteenth century. It had taken root as far back as the 1780s, when people began to link alcohol abuse to violence and to men who left their families or their jobs. The idea of moderation or all-out temperance gathered influence in the 1830s when churches and religious groups began to promote it, but it died out during the Civil War. Temperance organizations returned in the 1870s, however, most notably with the crusaders of the Woman's Christian Temperance Union.

In the 1890s, the idea of prohibition had taken hold, not just with moralists and religious leaders, but also among wide and disparate sections of the population nationwide, all of which had their own reasons for disliking alcohol or the people who were associated with it. Some linked it to gambling, prostitution, loose morals, corruption and other forms of crime. Doctors and progressive reformers who wanted to improve the lives of everyday people saw banning alcohol as a way to help. The Ku Klux Klan and ultra-right-wing nationalists saw Prohibition as a way to financially damage the German and Irish immigrants who had built the liquor business in the United States. Union leaders were torn. While saloons served as meeting halls and booze acted as a kind of labor movement lubricant, whiskey and beer were also causing widespread problems among the working class. And finally, women, who still weren't allowed to vote at the time—and weren't allowed in saloons—didn't mind the notion of Prohibition either.

In 1893, many of these groups, along with the Catholic Church and several Protestant denominations, joined together under the banner of an organization called the Anti-Saloon League to push individual cities, states and territories to ban alcohol one by one.

The saloonkeepers fought back, as did the breweries, on both a state and federal level. The United States Brewers Association had a vigilance committee that kept careful track of the goings on in cities and states across the country when it came to political pressure and who was voting to go "dry" and who wasn't. The group met regularly to discuss ways to counter the temperance movement, but it underestimated the forces at play.

In Colorado, the saloonkeepers underestimated women in particular. That half of the population had finally gained the right to vote Colorado in 1893—the second state in the country to do so—and many women got to work right away, organizing efforts to ostracize people who entered taverns and putting pressure on politicians to do the same. That change built on virulent nationalistic sentiments, anti-German feelings in particular, due to the tensions leading up to and during World War I, and labor unrest that was tied to taverns.

As a result, in November 1914, Colorado voters voted to ban the manufacture and sale of alcohol. The law went into effect on January 1, 1916, more than four years before the Eighteenth Amendment to the Constitution established Prohibition nationwide. Six other states, Arkansas, Idaho, Iowa, Oregon, South Carolina and Washington, went dry the same day.

While the saloon operators were shocked, the state's twelve remaining brewery owners—many of them savvy businessmen—were ready to diversify. Two in particular, Adolph Coors and Adolph Zang, had served on the United States Brewers Association's vigilance committee, so they were able to see Prohibition coming sooner than other brewers. This likely led to Coors diversifying early on and may have played a role in the Zang family's decision to sell its brewery to the English syndicate.

To stay in business, Tivoli switched to making a cereal drink called Dash, while Zang began producing ice cream and a low alcohol near beer. Neef Brothers also began making a near beer called Snappy, and Capitol Brewing, which opened in 1910 as a latecomer in the industry, became a grain milling operation. Up in Golden, Coors had begun manufacturing cement and ceramics, as well as malted milk, which it marketed as a "healthful and nourishing" beverage for children several years earlier.

Still, on December 31, 1915, Coors was forced to dump its remaining beer, about 17,391 gallons, in Clear Creek. That night in Denver, police were on alert for a final night of drunken debauchery, and things started off a high level. One group of people held a "funeral" for John Barleycorn—a character from an old folk song who represented beer and whiskey—and paraded a camel through downtown to mark the coming of "dry" times. Drinkers at the Heidelburg Cafe sang "Last Night was the End of the World."

But many of the saloons—which would be out of business the next day—had gotten rid of most of their booze, and some ran out of alcohol early in the evening and were serving lemonade. By 11:30 p.m., newspapers reported only a small number of revelers remaining, and by midnight, the streets had gone completely quiet.

6

POST-PROHIBITION

Selling booze was illegal for nineteen years, but that didn't mean it was hard to get. In fact, there were any number of ways to follow your pleasure.

For starters, small amounts of alcohol were legal for medicinal purposes. In the months after Prohibition took effect, the state issued sixteen thousand prescription forms for doctors who "could prescribe four-ounce doses of liquor for needy patients with each form," *Denver Post* scribe Dick Kreck wrote in a 2009 story about booze history. Alcohol was also allowed for religious reasons, though one church was reprimanded for consuming four hundred gallons of "sacramental wine in a month," Kreck wrote.

In late 1916, the state relented to certain pressures by revising the law to allow people to import liquor from wet states for personal use. Individuals were allowed to apply for permits giving them the right to possess two pints of wine and twenty-four quarts of beer each month.

Colorado tightened up on these laws in 1918 after passage of the Volstead Act and the Eighteenth Amendment and in advance of national Prohibition implementation on January 17, 1920. But Prohibition is credited with almost single-handedly creating the mob as we know it today. Gangsters began running alcohol from Canada, South America and elsewhere while less sophisticated operations distilled their own whiskey and moonshine in the United States.

While Colorado didn't have the violent, high-profile drama of Al Capone and Lucky Luciano, it did have some of its own liquor-fueled gang warfare, as well the Smaldone family, who rose to the top of the pile when it came to illegal gambling and bootlegging.

Speakeasies multiplied despite the constant threat of raids and the possibility of being poisoned by poorly made moonshine. At the Buckhorn Exchange, which the Neef brothers once owned, there was a secret staircase going up to a hidden room where the beer still flowed. Out front, "bakers" sold bottles of booze in hollowed out loaves of bread.

Prohibition didn't do much for the real estate market either. Some of the buildings that had housed taverns in Denver and elsewhere were taken over by grocery stores, ice cream parlors, restaurants, billiards and gaming houses. But many remained vacant.

Prohibition cost thousands of jobs in Colorado when it was enacted in 1916, and former saloon and brewery workers would periodically march in the streets to complain or demand work. Nationally, Prohibition cost tens of thousands of jobs in 1919.

Slowly, through the aftermath of World War II and into the Roaring '20s, the stock market collapse, the Dust Bowl, and the Great Depression, America realized not only that it could use a drink, but that Prohibition wasn't working. In fact, it was making things worse.

So, when Franklin D. Roosevelt was elected president in 1932 on a "wet" platform, Congress immediately began taking action to eliminate it, proposing a Twenty-First Amendment to the Constitution that would do away with the Eighteenth. Doing so would require the approval of three-fourths, or thirty-six, of the states. Colorado was the twenty-fourth state to ratify the proposed amendment on September 26, 1933, but Utah (ironically) sealed the deal in December 1933, officially ending what had been called the "noble" experiment by FDR's predecessor, Herbert Hoover.

To get people back to work earlier at breweries, saloons and liquor stores, though, Congress voted to raise the amount of alcohol allowed in what it considered to be "non-intoxicating" near beer from 0.5 percent alcohol by weight, which is what the limit had been during Prohibition, to 3.2 percent. FDR signed off on this bill, the Cullen-Harrison Act, in March 1933, and it became law on April 7.

That same day, thousands of people gathered at breweries around the country, hoping to get their first taste of legally produced beer in nearly a decade and a half. In Colorado, Coors had been busy brewing since March, and on April 7, it loaded a train with eighteen cars full of 3.2 percent beer and shipped it to Colorado's eager residents.

Coors produced malted milk during Prohibition, as well as cement and ceramics. *Coors Brewing.*

To prepare for the arrival of full-strength beer, wine and spirits, Colorado created its own liquor code in August 1933, "regulating the manufacture and sale of alcoholic liquor containing more than 3.2 percent of alcohol by weight." While cities and towns could elect to remain dry if they wanted to (and many, like Boulder, did for decades), they had to follow the new state code if they chose to allow the manufacture and sale of beer, wine and spirits.

The rules were also set up to try to keep the criminal element or the mob, which had been so prevalent during Prohibition, from controlling the liquor business. For instance, one clause read, "It shall be unlawful for any owner, part owner, share holder or person interested in any retail liquor store, to conduct, own, either in whole or in part, or be directly or indirectly interested in any other retail liquor store in this State." In other words, one person couldn't own multiple liquor stores.

That law is the reason why grocery chains—up until 2019—were only allowed to have one location selling anything stronger than 3.2 beer. It is also what paved the way for so many small craft breweries to be able to flourish many decades later. Since the chains weren't a factor, breweries, even tiny ones, could sell beer individually to each store as they saw fit. The result was a proliferation of beers and styles and breweries.

But lawmakers at the time still remembered the social and moral problems that led to Prohibition in the first place. They were also cognizant of the control that the breweries had exerted over saloons and taverns before Prohibition took effect.

To keep both from happening again, they made liquor sales illegal on Sundays (a rule that didn't change until 2008) and on Election Day so politicians couldn't trade booze for votes as they had done in years past. Lawmakers also created what became known as the three-tier system, in which liquor manufacturers, wholesalers and retail outlets each had to operate independently, and none were able to have a financial interest in the other.

But the Cullen-Harrison Act meant that 3.2 percent "non-intoxicating" beer was legal everywhere, even in dry towns, cities and states, though it could be regulated. The result was a complicated set of rules in many states governing each form of alcohol.

In Colorado, supermarkets and convenience stores were allowed to sell 3.2 percent beer in every location. In addition, people older than eighteen could drink it (at least until 1987 when lawmakers raised the age to twenty-one). Clubs that served only 3.2 percent beer were open to minors, although they had to close earlier than regular bars, and people could drink it in the city's parks. The law would mystify people for decades and continued to wreak havoc into 2019.

Coors, despite losing its founder in 1929, had managed to stay open with a combination of ingenuity and grit. But most of the other breweries that had been around when Colorado banned booze in 1916 didn't fare as well. Of the twelve that had tried to keep their doors open by making other products, only four succeeded: Coors, Tivoli Brewing in Denver, Walter Brewing in Pueblo, and Ph. Schneider Brewing in Trinidad.

Zang closed in 1927 and was put up for auction. Parts of it burned down, while some sections were occupied over the years by a dairy and a furniture warehouse, among other concerns. By 1968, both smokestacks had been torn down, and in 1983, the stables were leveled. Only two buildings from the compound are left today. One, located at the on-ramp to I-25, is the beautiful brewmasters house, which is now used for offices. The other building, located closer to REI on the same side of Water/Seventh Street, was a boardinghouse for Zang employees, called the Rocky Mountain Hotel.

It has been the home of various businesses over the years, including El Señor Sol Mexican restaurant, a dispensary, a bar and Confluence Kayaks.

Capitol Brewing, which had been located at Thirty-Eighth and Wazee Streets, just blocks from where Black Shirt Brewing is now, closed in 1917 and later burned down.

Neef Brothers also closed in 1917. Fred and Max, now in their golden years, were wealthy and established, and when their near-beer product didn't go over well, they retired. The brewery later became a radium processing facility and then a Superfund site. It was cleaned up in the early '90s and is now used as a warehouse, although only one story remains.

Nationwide, of the 1,100 or breweries that were in existence in the United States just one year before Prohibition, only about a third were able to open their doors again afterward, according to Brewers Association numbers.

And the country was changing. Not only had it been stitched closer together by radio broadcasts, film, baseball, automobile travel along the beginnings of the U.S. Highway System and even commercial airlines, but technological advancements also continued at a dizzying pace. Many, like frozen dinners and televisions, were in the home. As a result, consumer products companies helped create rapid homogenization, especially in food and beverages, from coast to coast. These changes began happening even faster after World War II when servicemen returned home and started having families and moving to the suburbs.

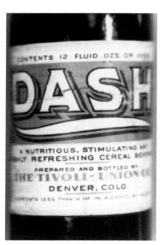

During Prohibition, Tivoli Brewing made a non-alcoholic beer called Dash. *Corey Marshall.*

For the beer companies, it was a dogfight. Coors and Tivoli competed head to head in Colorado, but their biggest rivals were out-of-state breweries like Wisconsin's Schlitz, Missouri's Anheuser-Busch and New Jersey's Ballantine, which were the top three sellers in 1950. Other regional powerhouses of the day included Pabst, Rheingold, Schaefer, Falstaff, Miller, Blatz and Pfeiffer. But unlike today, none of these breweries had more than 5 or 6 percent of the total U.S. beer market.

That would change in the ensuing decades as the famous old names—many founded by German immigrants—continued to buy one another out, resulting in rapid consolidation in the industry. Schlitz, for instance, sold to Stroh Brewery, which was in turn acquired by

Pabst Brewing. Pabst, which is now owned by an international investment conglomerate, also controls the rights to Blatz, Ballantine, Lone Star, Olympia, Falstaff, Rainier, Schaefer and Schmidt, among others. Still more breweries and brands, including Latrobe, Meisterbrau, Iron City, Olympia, Lucky, Old Style, Narragensett and many more also changed hands, sometimes repeatedly through the years.

Anheuser-Busch, meanwhile, grew rapidly by pushing its own brands, which included Budweiser, Busch, Natural Light and Michelob.

By the early 1960s, Colorado's two remaining breweries, Coors and Tivoli, were both thriving. Tivoli commissioned a $1 million expansion to keep up with demand for its Hi-En Brau brand while Coors was pioneering the use of aluminum cans.

In 1965, Loraine Good, John Good's daughter-in-law who had inherited the company in 1931 from John's son, John Edward, died, triggering a huge legal battle between the people who wanted her money. Tivoli was eventually sold to Carl and Joseph Occhiato, part of a family in Pueblo who owned a bottling plant and a beer distributorship. The brothers immediately introduced several successful beers, including Denver Beer, Aspen Gold and Mile-Hi.

But later that year, a huge Denver flood devastated the company. Then, on January 31, 1966, the Teamsters Local 435 and the Operating Engineers Local No. 1, unhappy with their contract and the new owners, went on strike and called for a statewide boycott of Tivoli beers. Although the Occhiatos were able to work through both of these setbacks, the business never recovered. Tivoli Brewing closed in 1969, leaving Coors as Colorado's last brewer.

That same year, Coors produced six million barrels of beer, all of which were sold in the same eleven-state region that the brewery had developed after Prohibition. By 1977, Coors had become the nation's fifth-largest brewery, and by 1979, it was making 13 million barrels of beer per year—all with that famous Rocky Mountain Spring Water.

And although profits were high, the decade marked a race to the bottom when it came to old-world brewing traditions, styles, variety and choice. Gone were the märzens and bocks of the past. What the remaining breweries had created were lighter lagers that resembled pilsners but were more of a watered-down amalgamation of styles, says Rose. They were backed by slick advertising campaigns that blasted over televisions and radios.

Coors, which had made only one brand, Banquet, for the previous two decades, introduced Coors Light in 1978, amid a wave of increasingly popular lower-calorie beers that would continue to value market share and image over quality and taste.

By 1979, there were just forty-two breweries in the United States operating a total of eighty plants, and industry analysts suggested that the number would drop to five by 1990.

But then something crazy happened.

The same year that the number of breweries reached an all-time low of forty-two and Coors's production reached an all-time high, two astrophysicists at the University of Colorado in Boulder—just twenty miles north of Golden—opened a forty-third brewery. It was tiny. It made murky English-style ales, and it helped inspire a beer revolution that hasn't slowed down since.

7

CHARLIE PAPAZIAN AND
THE CRAFT BEER REVOLUTION

In December 2017, the Smithsonian's National Museum of American History collected a prized artifact: a well-worn, eighteen-inch-long wooden spoon. Described as being notched for easy measuring and stained dark with a well-worn end, the utensil wasn't made by an ancient culture or used to cook for one of the signers of the Declaration of Independence. Rather, it belonged to the founding father of American homebrewing.

Born in 1949 in New Jersey, Charlie Papazian could have been a nuclear engineer. In fact, that's what he went to school to do at the University of Virginia, earning his degree in nuclear engineering in 1972. But Papazian was destined to take another, more effervescent path. In 1973, he got a hankering to go west and headed to Boulder because he knew someone there whose couch he could crash on if need be.

It was there that he planted the seeds that would later blossom into the homebrewing movement and help inspire the $28 billion craft brewing industry, which by the end of 2019, included more than eight thousand breweries making 27 million barrels of beer annually. Boulder is still home to the American Homebrewers Association (AHA) and the Brewers Association (BA)—the trade group representing the majority of the nation's craft breweries. Papazian created both of them, along with the Institute for Brewing Studies, the Great American Beer Festival (GABF), the World Beer Cup and *Zymurgy* magazine. He is also responsible for helping to create and manage the beer style guidelines that are commonly in use today in the United States.

Charlie Papazian was teaching homebrewing classes in Boulder in the 1970s. *Brewers Association.*

But Boulder's beer cred goes further than that. The town is also the birthplace of Boulder Beer Company, which is the oldest craft brewery in Colorado and, at the time, just the forty-third brewery in the country. Founded in a goat shed in 1979 by two astrophysicists at the University of Colorado, Boulder Beer persisted through many ups and downs before, sadly, announcing in January 2020 that it would sell its building and close its doors. (A separate brewery, Sleeping Giant, plans to make and sell some of Boulder Beer's brands.)

Boulder Beer, along with the BA and the AHA, would go on to change not just Colorado's eating and drinking culture and industries but also those of the entire country.

But it began with Charlie. Once he'd settled in Boulder, Papazian got a job teaching kindergarten and restarted a hobby he'd taken up three years earlier with a college friend: homebrewing. Although the practice wasn't technically legal—it wouldn't be until President Jimmy Carter signed legislation in 1978 making it acceptable to brew your own beer—most people ignored that fact, and Papazian began teaching homebrewing classes in his apartment and later in a classroom space.

He started by using a set of typed two-page homebrewing instructions— augmented by written notes—and eventually expanded to a six-page syllabus and then a seventy-eight-page self-published guide that he called "The Joy of Homebrewing." (The original two pages are now at the Smithsonian, along with the spoon. In 2017, the Smithsonian's National Museum of American History hired a historian to begin collecting artifacts and researching the role beer has played in U.S. history; as of late 2019, a small exhibit had opened as well.)

Papazian quickly developed a following. His smart and quietly charming personality combined with an almost evangelical enthusiasm for both brewing and drinking created an aura that people wanted to be around. The hobby also appealed to people who appreciated the do-it-yourself ethic that arose in the 1960s and '70s.

In his book about the history of the U.S. craft beer revolution, *The Audacity of Hops*, author Tom Acitelli writes that "Papazian earned a reputation in those early Boulder days as 'a magnet,'…a sort of amiable bearded eccentric who might organize a marbles tournament or a pig roast for hundreds of his closest friends."

Charlie Papazian stepped away from the Brewers Association in 2019 after forty years. *Brewers Association.*

Some of Papazian's students at the time included Russell Schehrer, who would go on to be the founding brewer at Wynkoop Brewing, which opened in 1988, and Jeff Lebesch, who cocreated New Belgium Brewing in 1991.

By 1974, Papazian and his merry band of misfits decided to throw a rager in the foothills west of Boulder. Fed by their own homebrew, Papazian and three hundred homebrewing students and friends built a stage for music, trucked in snow to keep their beer cold and gathered in tents for camping. The first Beer and Steer, as it was called, was a success, and Papazian and his friends continued the tradition for a decade, until GABF came along.

But it wasn't all just partying. In 1978, Papazian and a former homebrewing student, fellow schoolteacher Charlie Matzen, decided to get serious, well, sort of serious. Homebrewing had enough momentum, they figured, to support a magazine dedicated to the craft. So, with a grand total of $4,000, they published their first issue of *Zymurgy* in December 1978. Subscribers who paid $4 also became members of the American Homebrewing Association, which the two created, and for an extra $2, they received a copy of Papazian's self-published book.

"For all of us in '70s, it was the discovery of making beer at home and the excitement of finding new flavors and varieties," Papazian says. The idea that people could make a living by opening a brewery was a remote thought at the time—one that didn't come about "until we started drinking too much of our own homebrew."

The new law allowing for homebrewing went into effect on February 1, 1979. And although that made it easier for homebrewers to "come out of the closet," Papazian says, "the fact that it wasn't legal didn't really phase us at the time."

David Hummer and Rudolph "Stick" Ware weren't phased either. Ware, a PhD student at University of Colorado's Joint Institute for Laboratory Astrophysics, has been homebrewing since he was in high school in California. Hummer, who was the chairman of the department, was also experienced. The two had been thrilling other grad students with their beer at CU parties and eventually started joking around about starting a brewery.

It wasn't something that anyone did in the United States anymore. The year before, in 1978, the number of breweries nationwide had fallen to what would be an all-time, post-Prohibition low of 89, and then to 42 in 1979, down from 859 in 1941. Beginning in the 1950s, at least 5 breweries closed or were bought out every year. Many people believed that the number would eventually drop to fewer than 5.

Boulder Beer's David Hummer bottles beer for his new startup brewery. *Boulder Beer Company.*

But Ware and Hummer didn't necessarily know that, so on September 25, 1979, the two, along with a third partner named Al Nelson (an engineer) began brewing beer in a glorified goat shed on Nelson's family farm in the countryside near the town of Hygiene, which is in Boulder County about ten miles north of town. Boulder Brewing Company (now called Boulder Beer Company) began with a porter, which continued to be produced as Planet Porter until 2013, when it was finally put to bed in the face of changing craft beer trends. The owners, along with brewmaster Otto Zavatone, also made a stout and an English-style pale ale.

When Papazian heard about the place through friends, he jumped at the chance to visit. After all, there were only two other small breweries in the country that weren't making light lagers and weren't owned by big companies—Anchor in San Francisco and New Albion in Sonoma, California. And now there was one right there in Boulder.

Papazian had started holding a gathering around what he was calling the National Homebrew Competition, although up until that point, it had only attracted one entry from outside Colorado. But in 1981, he convinced the brewers from Boulder Beer and Portland's Cartright Brewing, along with Michigan brewing advocate Tom Burns, to come by to talk and mingle.

It proved to be a good mix. "All the homebrewers were gaga over listening to people who had seen their dream materialize," Papazian says.

That, and fortuitous meetings with international beer writer Michael Jackson at both the National Homebrewers Conference the year before and the Great British Beer Festival, convinced Papazian that he needed to start a beer festival for commercial breweries in the United States. Not that there were many commercial breweries.

Would it work? Like always, Papazian was confident in the face of long odds. "I was enthusiastic, and I surrounded myself with people who supported the ideas I had and who wanted to participate in the development of fun things," he says.

The first Great American Beer Festival took place from 4:30 to 9:30 p.m. on June 4, 1982, at Boulder's Hilton Harvest House. There were forty-seven beers from twenty-four breweries, including Anchor Steam, August Schell, Blitz-Weinhard, Boulder Beer, Coors, Falstaff, F.X. Matt, Latrobe, Leinenkugel, Rainier, River City, Sierra Nevada and Yuengling.

Fred Eckhardt, a legendary beer writer, homebrewer and beer historian who died in 2015, was at that fest, and he reminisced about it in a 2006 article published in *All About Beer* magazine: "The beer list was short by

The second annual GABF in 1983 was a bit of a free-for-all. *Photo courtesy of Brewers Association Archive.*

today's standards, but a revolutionary step forward for that bygone era," he wrote. "At that time, there were 78 brewing plants owned by the 40 U.S. brewing companies. Of those, 15 were considered 'small,' producing fewer than 100,000 barrels annually. Five of these outfits were what we would call 'craft' or 'micro,' four of which were entered into competition."

Eckhardt tried every beer that he hadn't sampled previously, while some other attendees tried them all. It took about an hour or an hour and half to get through them.

One of the participating breweries was Coors, which used the occasion to debut a new, fuller-flavored beer called George Killian's. "That was the first time it was tasted by the public, and they were excited to participate," Papazian says.

But Papazian and festival cofounders Frank Morris, Tom Burns and Stuart Harris didn't invite any other large beermakers, not because they didn't like them, but because "they didn't have any interesting beers," he says. "Coors was the only one. We didn't want a festival with a bunch of light lagers. We wouldn't have been able to sell tickets to a festival like that, at least we didn't think so at the time."

Jeff Brown is one of the lucky few who can say that he was at that very first festival. The managing partner of Jose Muldoon's, a Mexican restaurant in Boulder, Brown had developed a large beer list, so when Daniel Bradford, who was a waiter at Jose Muldoon's, approached him with the idea of being a sponsor, Brown took him up on it (Bradford later became marketing director for the AHA). Brown has long since lost the tasting notes he wrote down that day, but he says the festival was a lot of fun.

"These were long before the days of one-ounce pours, like they have today, so everyone was walking around with half-full glasses," he says. Brown had already met Papazian at a party and again when he took a class that Papazian offered on beer styles and flavors, and he says he was the perfect person to create GABF. "He's a great guy. He loves beer and he knew how to put on a good party. It served him well."

The following year, 1983, Papazian created the Institute for Brewing and Fermentation Studies to help commercial brewers and the Association of Brewers (which changed its name to the Brewers Association in 2005) as an umbrella organization for the institute and the American Homebrewers Association.

With Bradford's help, Papazian also found a publisher for *The Complete Joy of Homebrewing*, which Avon Books printed in 1984. In it, Papazian covered the history of beer, discussed brewing styles, presented lessons on how to brew and included several recipes. Throughout, he advises readers that brewing is easy, saying, "Relax. Don't Worry. Have a Homebrew." The book, now in its fourth edition, is the best-selling homebrewing manual ever.

By the third fest in 1984, GABF had outgrown the Hilton Harvest House in Boulder, or rather, "they disinvited us," Papazian says with a laugh, so the event moved to Denver's Currigan Exhibition Hall, the city's main exhibit space. But Papazian and his team had severely overestimated Denver's interest in the event, and although GABF attracted nearly three thousand people, it was an embarrassingly small number for the space.

So Papazian pulled back for a few years after that, holding the festival at a variety of venues, including the Regency Hotel and the Merchandise Mart, both in Denver. "We were way ahead of our time. But we survived and learned how to grow things slowly and organically," he adds.

In 1987, the Association of Brewers instituted official GABF style guidelines for the first time—for twelve different styles—and a blind tasting panel for awards. Papazian and the BA would continue to add to that list every year. (By 2018, 2,200 different breweries entered more than 8,300 beers in a whopping 102 categories.)

The Great American Beer Festival in 2017; it still inspires mania in Denver. *Brewers Association.*

The tenth festival, in 1994, was held at the Denver Merchandise Mart where seven thousand people tried five hundred beers from 150 breweries. From there, it moved back to Currigan and finally to the Colorado Convention Center, which replaced Currigan in 2000.

Although it had taken a while, by that time, microbrews had finally caught on in Denver. In 1988, a full nine years after Boulder Brewing kicked things off, John Hickenlooper and his partners opened Wynkoop Brewing, the second small brewery in the state. It was followed by more than a dozen other breweries over the next three years, including Odell, Old Colorado, New Belgium and CooperSmith's in Fort Collins; Breckenridge Brewing in Breckenridge, Durango and Carver in Durango; Champion and Rock Bottom in Denver; and the Walnut Brewery in Boulder.

Those last two, Walnut and Rock Bottom, were created by longtime Boulder restaurant entrepreneurs Frank and Gina Day, who founded the Old Chicago pizza taproom chain in 1976 and owned Jose Muldoon's, where Brown worked.

They opened the Walnut Brewery in 1989, so when Boulder Brewing fell on hard times in 1990, the ownership group approached the Days and

Left to right: Boulder Beer brewmaster David Zuckerman, GABF director Nancy Johnson and former Boulder Beer president Jeff Brown in 2016. *Jonathan Shikes*

One of Boulder Beer's first bottles, along with several GABF commemorative editions. *Jonathan Shikes.*

asked if they wanted to buy it. The original owners, Hummer, Ware and Nelson, had taken the company public in the early 1980s and later left the business, which now faced bankruptcy. The Days renamed it Boulder Beer Company and brought in Brown to run it with David Zuckerman, who had been brewmaster at Bridgeport Brewing in Portland. Gina Day was still the majority owner when Boulder Beer announced in 2020 that it would close.

By then, there were 284 breweries in the United States, and Papazian had turned the Association of Brewers into a professionally run, not-for-profit association—and became a sort of folk hero along the way.

On January 23, 2019, his seventieth birthday, Papazian retired from the BA, although he is still working on several beer-related projects and visiting new Colorado breweries almost every month. "Forty years is a long time to be with one organization," he says. "I'll see what comes next."

8

JOHN HICKENLOOPER

THE MAYOR OF LODO

Pasted to the walls at Wynkoop Brewing are hundreds of old brew sheets representing nearly thirty years of brewing beer. Most are initialed by the head brewers. There's RS for Russell Schehrer, a cofounder and the first brewer; TD for Tom Dargen, who brewed there for eleven years, and KK for Kyle Karstens, who learned under Dargen. Some of the later brewers, like Thomas Larsen, Andy Brown, Mike Sims and Bess Dougherty, who became the first woman to brew at Wynkoop, aren't the walls yet, but they might be added later.

There's no JH, though. That's because Wynkoop's most famous employee and its cofounder—John Hickenlooper—never brewed the beer. But it's safe to say that Hickenlooper, who finished his second term as Colorado governor at the end of 2018 before launching a short-lived presidential campaign in 2019 and a senatorial campaign later that year, did more to grow and promote small breweries in Colorado than any other person in history. But his influence extended beyond brewing. Hickenlooper's energy, vision, magnetism and tolerance for risk changed the entire city—and that was before he even entered politics.

Hickenlooper's story has been told many times, perhaps most thoroughly in his 2016 autobiography *The Opposite of Woe: My Life in Beer and Politics*, but it never seems to get old, perhaps because there is always a new story, a fresh angle, a fascinating piece of trivia.

It began in 1952, in Narberth, Pennsylvania, where Hickenlooper—"a goofy mouthful of a thing to say," as Hickenlooper acknowledges in his book—was born. He was the youngest of four kids, to John and Anne, or Hick and Shrimpy as they were called. His father died when Hickenlooper was just eight years old, leaving his mother to raise the kids alone.

When he was eighteen, Hickenlooper enrolled at Wesleyan University in Connecticut, where he graduated in 1974 with a degree in English literature before earning his master's degree a few years later in environmental science. It was during this time that he first learned how to homebrew during a summer school-building project in Maine.

Later, in the summer of 1981, Hickenlooper moved to Denver and took a job with Buckhorn Petroleum, an oil and gas company, where he stayed for five years until the oil glut of the 1980s forced a crisis in the industry and thousands of layoffs. Hickenlooper was one of the cuts.

It was the best thing that could have happened. Hickenlooper turned his attention to his other love at the time, writing. But he also used his severance pay to buy a 1967 red Chevy Malibu and headed west with a friend to visit his brother Sydney in Berkeley, California. There, he spent an evening at the Triple Rock Brewery and Alehouse, which had just opened. The place was a novelty—it made and served its own beer.

"There was a line out the door and halfway down the block. On a weeknight! I thought, 'You've got to be kidding me.' I was excited to taste what all the fuss was about," Hickenlooper writes in his autobiography. "I ordered a beer and couldn't believe the flavor," he continues. "Compared with the usual beers I drank, this one was richer and less carbonated, smoother and softer on the palate, and with a real bouquet. I thought to myself, 'I would have driven twenty minutes out of my way without thinking twice about it to have a beer or two like this.'"

Within a few months, Hickenlooper had drafted another former geologist and friend, Jerry Williams, into a plan to open their own brewpub in Denver. It would serve fresh, high-quality beer and food and offer customers a chance to look in on the brewing equipment itself as they imbibed.

"There was nothing between New York and California, no brewpubs. We were the first," Hickenlooper says. "There's an old expression, 'Pioneers take the arrows, settlers take the land.' And we did take some arrows. But we did it the right way. We weren't just trying to make money. We had a purpose—to reinvent a great American product."

So, with the same mixture of naiveté and smarts, energy and irreverence, spontaneity and vision that would characterize almost everything he did over the following two decades, Hickenlooper set about raising money, gathering goodwill and formulating a business plan.

John Hickenlooper at the height of the Wynkoop's popularity in 1993. *David Bjorkman/ Brewers Association Archive.*

But first, he found a brewer. Russell Schehrer was a charming, if sometimes difficult and eccentric choice. A computer programmer, painter, and man whose wild reputation preceded (and now follows) him, Schehrer was also a master homebrewer. He had won the Homebrewer of the Year Award in 1985 from Charlie Papazian's American Homebrewers Association and came highly recommended by Papazian himself. Schehrer, who died in 1996 at the age of thirty-eight, is now memorialized by the Russell Schehrer Award for Innovation in Craft Brewing. He was among the first U.S. microbrewers to make mead, cider, doppel alt, cream stout and chili beer.

Then they found a location—the five-story J.S. Brown Mercantile Building at the corner of Eighteenth and Wynkoop Streets. Built in 1899 as a wholesale grocery warehouse, the gorgeous red-brick building had ornate arched windows, pressed-tin ceilings and sandstone trim. In another neighborhood, and in another era, it would have cost a fortune to lease 11,600 square feet of space on the ground floor of that building. But in 1988, it cost one dollar per square foot. That's because the building was located on the sketchy—some might have even said scary—north end of downtown Denver, surrounded by vacant buildings, empty lots and homeless camps. It was also across the street from Union Station and the city's railroad tracks.

A century earlier, in the time of Denver's first brewers, like John Good, Moritz Sigi and Philip Zang, this area had been Denver's beating heart. Union Station, which had at one time been the hub that brought just about everything and everyone in and out of the city, now only catered to a few sad Amtrak customers and skiers heading to Winter Park. Its famed neon "Travel by Train" sign usually displayed a few letters that blinked or had gone dark.

Although the neighborhood was beginning to show some of the tiniest signs of life, no one could have imagined how it would change in just a few short years. In late 1988, the city announced that if Major League Baseball awarded Denver a team, the new ballpark would be located just two blocks away, along Twentieth Street. When the stadium was built in 1995, Lower Downtown, or LoDo as Denver Post columnist Dick Kreck coined it, was already exploding with development. Empty buildings became restaurants, bars, stores and condos. Vacant lots were filled with cars or new construction. Today, Union Station, which has been redeveloped into a multimillion-dollar eating and drinking center and hotel is once again the beating heart of Denver.

John Hickenlooper was at the middle of it all.

But in 1987, as he tried to gather investors, the corner of Eighteenth and Wynkoop Streets didn't look like much. After being rejected by thirty-two banks, he finally got a pair of bank loans and raised the rest of the money from thirty-five private investors, mainly friends and family, including Scherher and his then-wife, Barbara McFarlane; Williams and his wife, Martha; and Wynkoop landlord Jack Barton. Then he cobbled together furniture, kitchen equipment, glassware and some old toilets that were being scrapped by a nearby hotel. Hickenlooper also found a chef, Mark Schiffler, who would become one of the six founding partners.

Opening day was scheduled for October 18, 1988, and Hickenlooper was already displaying the marketing savvy that would come to define him: beers, he told the *Denver Post*'s Kreck, would be sold at the pre-Prohibition price of twenty-five cents on that day. It worked—maybe a little too well. A line formed around the block before the doors opened. All the television stations and newspapers were there. Even the mayor showed up.

The place was an immediate success. "By our second month we were earning a profit; suddenly there was money in our account. Eighteen months after opening we had retired our bank debt and a third of the rest of our debt," Hickenlooper writes in his book.

"Things were crazy back then," says Tom Dargen, who took a job as a busboy at the Wynkoop a month after it opened. He was a beer lover

Wynkoop Brewing opened in the J.S. Brown Mercantile Building in 1988 and is still going strong today. *Jonathan Shikes.*

finishing his degree in history at the University of Colorado at Denver and was in need of extra cash. Dargen had grown up in Portland and then Denver, drinking Sierra Nevada and Boulder Beer, courtesy of his mom, from the time he was thirteen or fourteen. "I was smitten, but I didn't think you could actually get a job making beer." But that's what happened.

A few months after starting, Dargen was offered a job as a congressional aide in Washington, D.C., but he didn't want to leave, so he asked McFarlane if he could work behind the bar—a better, higher-paying gig. At the time, the place was jumping, packed every night, and McFarlane said there were no openings at the bar, but Schehrer needed some help in the brewery. "I had never brewed before, but wearing a tie wasn't nearly as attractive as those rubber boots, so I took it," Dargen says. "Within six months I was pretty much running the brewery."

One of the biggest, earliest disputes was over the beer itself.

"Russell had an inability to belch, so he didn't care for American fizzy yellow beers," Dargen remembers. As a result, the Wynkoop only brewed English-style cask ales—an ESB, a porter, a pale ale—which are typically uncarbonated and served at around fifty-five degrees Fahrenheit. "Warm and flat is where it's at," read the signs on the wall that Shehrer installed. "In Russ we trust," read the T-shirts that Schehrer's supporters made.

But the rest of the partners wanted something colder, lighter and carbonated. After all, that's what beer had been for the better part of the past one hundred years—especially in Denver, which had grown up on German lagers—and that's what people expected. Although patrons had slurped it up on opening day, Dargen says many just didn't like warm and flat.

"John and Russell both had very strong personalities, and Jerry Williams was a real character, too. Eventually, John got tired of arguing with Russell about not having a cold carbonated beer, and he told me, 'I'll give you $1,000 if you can get cold carbonated beer behind the bar." Stories differ, but someone eventually persuaded Shehrer to begrudgingly allow it. The beer was an American wheat ale and was followed by a raspberry wheat, a style that was almost mandatory for breweries back then.

Dargen stayed on for the next eleven years (minus a six-month stint overseas) and watched the Wynkoop and Hickenlooper become famous. "In five years, we grew from a busy brewpub to being the biggest brewpub in the world. We were making everything under the sun, meads, ciders, fruit beers, field beers, and even our own vinegar—sometimes on purpose. It was great training for someone so young," says Dargen, whose title was manager of the liquids, "goofy titles for goofy times," he adds.

The parties, both on site and off, were legendary, as well. "There are stories for days," Dargen says—often filled with more vices than just beer and more reminiscent of the old West than the new. Some of these parties inspired the kinds of tall tales—whether true or fictional—that made people flock to Hickenlooper, and he evolved into the kind of outsized character that people in the West have always been drawn to. For his fortieth birthday in 1992, for instance, Hickenlooper sent invitations with a photo of him and a friend sitting on the Wynkoop's bar wearing nothing but bandanas, cowboy boots, serious expressions and well-placed cowboy hats. By the mid-'90s, Denver was Hicktown, and Hick was known as the mayor of LoDo.

One of the most epic sagas from the Wynkoop's past involved pigs. Each year, the brewpub celebrated its anniversary with a pig roast, and for the third anniversary, Hickenlooper came up with a harebrained scheme to get some pigs and race them down the alley behind the Wynkoop. The Running of the Pigs—or Pamplona on the Platte, as it was nicknamed—drew a good crowd. But it also drew the attention of animal activists.

"We got a nasty letter from the People for the Ethical Treatment of Animals, which also got us national press," recalls Dargen. "Those swine smelled of free publicity to John, and he convinced the PETA people that we weren't doing any harm to the pigs or making them run or squeal." Hickenlooper took the opportunity to grandly change the name to the Parade of Pigs and made the goal to see who could please their pig the most.

It was a doomed effort. "One year," Dargen says, "one of the pigs decided it didn't like being on a leash and it bolted. So, I remember chasing this squealing pig through the parking lot, all the while PETA is freaking out. I had to dive on it to capture it. It was classic Wynkoop."

Needless to say, Hickenlooper eventually did away with the pigs—but with the same media flare that defined him. In 2000, he hosted the first Prairie Preservation Day instead, an event created in partnership with the animal activists. The event included demonstrations on how prairie dogs help the ecosystem around them, and attendees got to try Prairie Pup Pale Ale and take home an "I Saved a Prairie Dog at the Wynkoop Brewing Co." souvenir glass.

His brewery tours were legendary as well, Dargen says, as Hickenlooper loved to tell off-color jokes. There was one about the "hiney lick" maneuver and another about a one-armed man counting his change, involving Hickenlooper putting his finger through his open fly to count the coins in his hand. And then there was the way that Hickenlooper explained why brewers have to keep their process sanitary when using yeast: "It's kind of like an orgy," he would tell any random group of grandmothers. "You don't want any uninvited guests."

Never afraid to use his somewhat ungainly appearance and goofy grin to market the brewery and the city as a whole, he once appeared on the Phil Donahue show and was a regular in the local media—always ready with a great quote. He is usually credited for originating Colorado's nickname, the Napa Valley of Craft Beer, and he made sure that reporters, editors and other journalists always got their first beer free.

"He was a political animal," Dargen says. "All the press people hung out there, and *Westword*'s offices were across the street for a decade. If you were a writer and you wanted a keg for your birthday or something there would rarely be a charge and it would likely be delivered to your house by him or more likely a brewer. We were whores. We gave away a lot of liquid. But that was a big reason why John became as well known and loved as he is."

Aside from *Westword* editor Patricia Calhoun and the *Denver Post*'s Kreck, dozens of other media types, along with politicians and local celebrities showed up at the Wynkoop on a regular basis. One of those was "retired" ad man, local character and occasional Hickenlooper collaborator Lew Cady. A rabble-rouser and beer lover who had a similar flare for marketing, Cady enjoyed recording "firsts" and "lasts" at local bars and breweries—the first paying customer at the first Rock Bottom in Denver, the first inside the Oskar Blues–owned Tasty Weasel, the first to drink all four beers on tap at Coors Field on the first day it opened. He'd continue recording firsts through 2012; Cady died in 2013.

Behind the antics, though, Hickenlooper oozed a calculated, if typically off-the-cuff, genius and a driving ambition that always had him focusing on the next big thing. In the early '90s, that took two forms: real estate investments in LoDo and investments in other brewpubs, both in Colorado and in other states.

In 1989, Hickenlooper teamed up with Scott Smith and Brad Page to open CooperSmith's Pub and Brewery in Fort Collins. Then he bought a building in Colorado Springs where he opened Phantom Canyon Brewing. After that, he invested and consulted in new brewpubs in Nebraska, Iowa, Wyoming, South Dakota, Kansas, Wisconsin, West Virginia, Kentucky and San Francisco. Each one had its own identity and investors, but not all of them worked—some failed quite spectacularly. So, Hickenlooper eventually sold his interest in those pubs and, over a decade or so, bought a variety of landmark restaurants in Denver, including the Wazee Supper Club, the Cherry Cricket, Gaetano's Italian and the Goosetown Tavern.

In 1991, he bought his building and converted the second story into a pool hall—a move done in part to compete with Rock Bottom Brewing and Champion Brewing, which both opened large brewpubs in Denver that year. Then he renovated the top three stories into condos, moving into one of them himself. Later, Hickenlooper and Tattered Cover Bookstore owner Joyce Meskis bought another historic building a few blocks away to house the store's new location. He was a partner on several large condo projects in LoDo and invested in other nearby buildings.

With the opening of Coors Field, annual revenues at Wynkoop jumped from $4 million to $8 million. Hickenlooper was making money, but he was always reinvesting in the city and making sure that journalists, lawmakers and the public knew what was best for beer (and what beer was best for them).

And what great beer it was. Though Schehrer left in the early '90s, Wynkoop continued to focus on English-style ales—beers that had never really been seen in Denver. Some of the earliest were St. Charles ESB,

Cowtown Milk Stout, London Calling IPA and the flagship Rail Yard Ale. Dargen first brewed Rail Yard Ale, an amber ale, to celebrate his wedding and named it after the train station across the street. "It took off. It became 40 percent of everything we brewed at the Wynkoop," Dargen says. "If I have a legacy, that's it."

Dargen left Wynkoop in 1999 to join the Gordon Biersch Brewery restaurant chain, and as the company grew and added new locations, he became a regional brewer and then the director of brewing operations. Years later, the company was purchased and merged with the Colorado-based Rock Bottom and Old Chicago chains to become CraftWorks Restaurants and Breweries. The irony is not lost on Dargen, who is now the vice-president of brewing operations for a company that was the Wynkoop's chief competitor.

Moving on proved to be a fortuitous decision. In 1999, Hickenlooper and Cady kicked off a grassroots campaign to preserve the name Mile High Stadium on the new home that was being built for the Denver Broncos. It quickly snowballed into a major initiative backed by the majority of the public. The campaign didn't really work, as the naming rights were sold to Invesco, but at least it stayed as part of the name, Invesco Field at Mile High.

The campaign worked for Hickenlooper, though. In 2001, he began fielding calls from people who thought he should run for mayor—and not just the mayor of LoDo. By that time, the Wynkoop's era as LoDo's number-one hotspot was already coming to an end, and Hickenlooper officially threw his hat in the political ring. He was elected as mayor in 2003 and again in 2007, resigning in 2011, when he was elected governor of Colorado. Hickenlooper again served two terms and by 2018 was being talked about as a potential presidential candidate.

Politics didn't leave a lot of room for pubs. In 2003, after becoming mayor, Hickenlooper put his business interests into a blind trust that was overseen by Lee Driscoll, one of his longtime business investors and partners. Driscoll and his family had helped finance the pub expansion in the '90s, and he served on the board of the larger company. In 2007, Driscoll and rest of the ownership decided to cash Hickenlooper out, selling his stake in the business for him for $5.8 million. The geologist turned publican turned mayor made a lot of money.

But he also made a lot of friends and a big difference for Denver. In 2010, while he was running for governor for the first time, Hickenlooper released his tax returns going all the way back to 1985. They showed that he earned more than $16 million over the time period, according to a story in the *Colorado Independent*. But they showed something else as well. In the

Then-governor John Hickenlooper celebrates his roots at the 2017 Great American Beer Festival. *Brewers Association Archive.*

same twenty-three-year period, Hickenlooper donated about $3 million in cash, stocks and real estate to various charitable causes. The first donation was in 1986.

None of that surprises Dargen.

Hickenlooper could be relentless and hard driving, but he was also endearing and magnetic. He could schmooze just about anyone but remain oddly distant with his closest friends.

"He could be a blast and he could be a pain the ass," Dargen explains. "But from the very early days, he was all about supporting charities and art galleries and political causes. It's something that set a standard and helped make craft beer what it is today."

And he always supported Dargen personally, writing checks or extending loans that helped him move, buy a house and pay for his son's medical expenses. "We weren't super close, but he was always there for me and he has been a big influence on my life."

9
EARLY CRAFT BEER PIONEERS

Denver is Colorado's largest city, its capital and heart, but to be honest, until recently, Denver was only the third, maybe even the fourth, best beer town in the state, and it wasn't even close. Boulder, thanks to Boulder Beer Company and Charlie Papazian, was craft beer's birthplace, and it developed a following very early on. Fort Collins, Boulder's fellow, albeit lesser known, college town about a half hour to the north was where the state's commercial brewing industry really developed, thanks partly to Odell Brewing and New Belgium Brewing. As of early 2019, these two pioneers were, respectively, the twenty-third- and fourth-largest craft brewers in the nation. (New Belgium sold to Japan's Kirin in late 2019, removing it from the list of independent craft breweries.)

But in 1989, when Doug and Wynne Odell were driving around Fort Collins looking for a place to start their planned brewery, there was really only one beermaker that people knew: Anheuser-Busch, which had opened a huge plant just north of town in 1988. In fact, when the Odells told a real estate broker about their plans, he responded by saying, "A brewery? But we already have one of those," Wynne recalls.

By the end of 1989, there would be three more.

Odell Brewing opened in a 1915 grain elevator, though it moved to larger digs five years later and has expanded several times since. Its first beer was Odell's Golden Ale, followed by 90 Shilling and Heartland Wheat. CooperSmith's Pub and Brewery also opened that year in Old Town Square, serving English ales. That brewery was founded by Scott Smith

Left to right: Corkie, Wynne and Doug Odell founded Odell Brewing in 1989. *Odell Brewing.*

and Brad Page, with assistance from John Hickenlooper. And finally, Joseph Neckel opened Old Colorado Brewing. Although it closed in the early 2000s, it was recently revived by Neckel's family members in the nearby town of Wellington.

In 1989, there were only a handful of other smaller breweries in the state, including Boulder Beer, Wynkoop Brewing and Carver Brewing, in Durango.

Doug, an entrepreneur, and Wynne, who was in banking, were living in Seattle when they decided to test their marriage by working together. And they decided that beer was the business they wanted to be in. The couple moved to Fort Collins, where Doug's sister, Corkie, lived because they thought Seattle was already oversaturated with breweries. It had six.

Doug was a homebrewer who had worked for Fritz Maytag at San Francisco's Anchor Brewing, and when he and Wynne were dating, they'd always go out for beers. It was something they both loved, and it seemed like a natural fit. So, with the money they got from selling their home in Seattle, and with loans from their parents and a few other investors (totaling just $135,000 in all), Doug, Wynne and Corkie found a space, bought a fifteen-barrel brewhouse from Specific Mechanical in Canada and went into business.

"Our aspirations were small," Wynne says. Doug was a fan of English-style ales, so that's what the brewery started with; 90 Shilling, still Odell's most well-known beer, was one of the first recipes he made. But Odell didn't package or serve food. Instead, the Odells sold kegs to local bars and offered one-gallon plastic "bladders" of beer that they sold out of the brewery. "Right away, people wanted to take tours and take beer with them," Wynne says.

Within a year, the brewery was profitable, and the Odells were able to pay off their loans—a financial decision that worked out well. Unlike many other breweries, the Odells kept full financial control of the brewery until 2015, when they sold 70 percent of the company through a combination of a management buyout and an employee stock ownership plan. They had shown that it could be done—normal people could create a successful brewery without much money. This paved the way for other would-be brewers.

But Doug Odell didn't just want to create a business; he wanted a community as well. So, in 1990, he and Brad Page, who had brewed at Wynkoop before moving to CooperSmith's in 1989, decided to start a festival. Modeled on the Oregon Brewers Festival, which Page had been to, the first Colorado Brewers' Festival took place in the summer of 1990 and included every brewery in the state—all eleven of them. In addition to Odell, Old Colorado and CooperSmith's, there was Boulder Beer, Wynkoop and Carver Brewing, along with three newbies, Breckenridge Brewery, Walnut Brewery and Durango Brewery. The big boys, Coors and Anheuser-Busch, also attended.

It was a turning point for the industry in the state. Not only did it solidify Fort Collins as an early hot spot for craft beer, but it was also the first time that all of the microbreweries in Colorado had gathered in one place at one time. Over the next few years, the festival would become a breeding ground for ideas, community and the camaraderie that has continued to define the craft brewing industry for twenty-five years. "Beer festivals were pretty darn new at the time, so it was the brewers pouring their own beer. That's what made it cool and gave it authenticity," Wynne says. "There was no marketing, no posters, no giveaways. Just beer."

And a lot of people appreciated that—people like Jeff Lebesch. Like many other people in the 1980s and '90s, Lebesch learned that there was a whole other world of beer by taking a trip overseas. The Fort Collins–area engineer took a now-legendary cycling trip across Belgium and returned with some crazy ideas about brewing Belgian-style beers in the United

States. Shortly thereafter, Lebesch and his wife, Kim Jordan, a social worker, started a brewery in their basement. They called it New Belgium Brewing in honor of his inspiration, and they named one of their beers Fat Tire to celebrate his mode of transportation.

At the time, CooperSmith's was doing "pub beer," and Odell was selling kegs, but no one in the area was bottling beer, Kim Jordan remembers. "There was the dawning of a realization among liquor store owners that they wanted to have something that people could buy and take home with them. It was a nice niche for us to be able to fill."

It caught on quickly. Lebesch and Jordan were overwhelmed by demand almost immediately and began self-distributing from the back of Jordan's car. They were also juggling full-time jobs and parenthood. Jordan would famously make deliveries while one of her children did homework in the car, and they printed their home phone number on their first beer labels—something that elicited plenty of drunk dials. By 1993, New Belgium was distributing bottles of Abbey Ale, Old Cherry and, of course, its flagship Fat Tire up and down the Front Range and in mountain towns, taking weekends to drop it off at stores.

"People certainly said we were crazy and that Fat Tire was a terrible name for a beer," Jordan remembers. But by naming the company New Belgium, they realized that they had license to make whatever they wanted and to try out new styles.

Belgian yeasts were new for American drinkers. "It was the rare beer aficionado who understood that that beer was distinctly its own," Jordan says. But they quickly adjusted. Abbey Ale won a gold medal in 1993 at the Great American Beer Festival and won more medals in 1995, 1996, 1997 and 1998. By then, breweries throughout Colorado and across the country were scrambling to make amber ales like Fat Tire.

In fact, it was malty ambers, ESBs and Scottish ales that "put Colorado on the map," says Steve Kurowski, the former spokesman for the Colorado Brewers Guild. He points to beers like Odell 90 Shilling, Bristol Brewing's Laughing Lab, Wynkoop's Rail Yard Ale, Oasis Scarab Red, Great Divide Arapaho Amber and Breckenridge's Avalanche Ale for pioneering these flavors.

Lebesch and Jordan didn't rest, though. They'd hired Peter Bouckaert, a promising Belgian brewer who'd worked at Rodenbach, the famed two-hundred-year-old Belgian sour beer maker, before starting and running his own brewery in Belgium for two years. At the time, New Belgium was Fat Tire, Sunshine Wheat, Old Cherry, Abbey and Trippel. So, when the

Kim Jordan turned New Belgium Brewing into the fourth-largest craft brewer in the nation. *New Belgium Brewing.*

brewery expanded and moved to a new location, Bouckaert added a few seasonals. Then, in 1997, he brewed a sour—a bold choice for an American brewery in that decade, when there were almost none.

La Folie, a classic Flanders-style sour brown aged in wooden barrels for one to three years, went on to become a standard for New Belgium, a frequent medal winner and one of the most highly rated sours in the United States. It also sparked the sour movement in America.

Lebesch backed away from day-to-day operations at New Belgium in 2000, shortly after he and Jordan divorced. But the floodgates had opened for craft beer in the rest of the state, and a couple dozen breweries tried their hand at it around the state, creating a new kind of beer culture, a new kind of beer drinker and a community around both.

In 1990, Old Chicago founder Frank Day opened Boulder's first brewpub (Boulder Beer didn't serve food at the time), the Walnut Brewery, just off the Pearl Street Mall. The Walnut closed in 2017, but it left a lasting legacy since Day used it as a model for the Rock Bottom chain, which he also started.

Oasis Brewing came next, in 1991, offering beers like Scarab Red, Tut Brown Ale and Zoser Stout—catchy names that grabbed the attention of microbrew drinkers around the state. Founder George Hanna closed Oasis in 2001 but reopened it in Denver in 2018, offering the same beers, which are now referred to as old-school styles.

The Boulder brewing scene would really kick off in 1993, though, with the opening of three breweries that would change the face of Colorado. The father-and-son duo of Larry and Adam Avery opened Avery Brewing in an office park in Boulder in 1993 and, a decade later, began breaking the mold in every way. Avery became known for its huge, boundary-busting beers, like Hog Heaven, a barleywine/IPA hybrid; Salvation Belgian Golden Ale; and The Beast, a 17 percent ABV Belgian strong dark ale. Avery moved to a $30 million, 5.6-acre campus in 2015 and was purchased by Spanish brewing giant Mahou San Miguel three years later.

The Mountain Sun Pub and Brewery, which embodies the iconoclastic, hippie vibe that makes Boulder what it is, was founded in 1993 by Kevin Daly. Today, the company includes five restaurants in Boulder, Denver and Longmont, three of which are also breweries. Mountain Sun also created Stout Month, which has become an iconic annual celebration of dark beers.

And finally, there was firefighter Gordon Knight, who opened High Country Brewery in Boulder in 1993 before moving it to Estes Park in 1994 and changing the name to Estes Park Brewing. Knight, who had a passion for hoppy beers, then opened Twisted Pine Brewing in Boulder in 1995 before selling to Bob Baile the next year. Baile had opened Peak to Peak Brewing in Rollinsville but decided to merge the two operations. Knight, a volunteer firefighter, died in 2002, when his helicopter crashed while he was battling a fire near Lyons. Oskar Blues now makes a beer, G'Knight Imperial Red IPA, dedicated to him. Twisted Pine, now a brewpub, was one of the first to use ingredients like coffee, chili peppers and fruit in its unusual beers.

Up the road in Longmont, Left Hand Brewing got its start in 1993, when two air force buddies, Dick Doore and Eric Wallace, opened a brewery on "the banks of the mighty St. Vrain." Now the fourth-largest craft brewery in Colorado—and the fiftieth largest in the country, as of 2018—Left Hand paved the way for several new styles, most notably packaged nitrogenated beer. Wallace, a vocal advocate of craft brewery independence, helped create the Colorado Brewers Guild and served as chairman of the Brewers Association in 2018.

Colorado's mountain towns also jumped in early. Breckenridge Brewery opened in the ski town of the same name in 1990 and was followed by Hubcap Brewery and Kitchen in Vail in 1991. Hubcap, now closed, was where many early Colorado brewers earned their chops. Flying Dog Brewery opened in Aspen in 1991 before moving to Denver in 1994 and then to Maryland in 2008. Heavenly Daze cranked up in Steamboat in 1992 before it also moved to Denver and later closed. There was also Crested Butte Brewing at the Idle Spur Pub, which turned out award-winning beers like Red Lady Ale and Buffalo Peace Ale, beginning in 1991.

Closer to Denver, geologists Charlie and Janine Sturdavant opened Golden City Brewing in Golden in 1993. Situated in a machine shop in their backyard, they jokingly called it the second-largest brewery in Golden. The next year, Charlie teamed up with Breckenridge's first brewmaster, the late Tim Lenahan, to create Tommyknocker Brewery in Idaho Springs, a brewpub that is still a must-stop for skiers returning from the mountains on I-70 in the winter.

Farther south, John Hickenlooper's team branched out into Colorado Springs in 1993 with Phantom Canyon Brewing. Bristol Brewing opened in Colorado Springs in 1994 and is now the wizened grandfather of the southern Front Range, having pioneered several styles. Its Laughing Lab Scottish Ale was ubiquitous throughout the state at one time.

The final major brewing center at the time was Durango, which has one of the oldest, strongest brewing scenes in Colorado, especially when you consider its small size.

Durango boasts some early pioneers, including Carver Brewing, which opened just months after Wynkoop in 1988, as the third craft brewery in Colorado, and Durango Brewing, which was founded in 1990 and has gone through several ownership changes. Ska Brewing set a new standard in 1995 when founders Dave Thibodeau and Bill Graham brought their ska/punk ethos and enormous senses of humor to town (a third owner, Matt Vincent, joined them later). Ska became just the second brewery in the country to can its beers in 2003 and now distributes in multiple states. Durango's Steamworks Brewing opened the same year as Ska.

In the mid-1990s, John Hickenlooper would coin (or at least popularize) the term "Napa Valley of Craft Beer" to describe the fertile stretch of breweries that developed along Colorado's Front Range in the 1990s. It's a fun moniker, but Denver beer publicist and philosopher Marty Jones thinks there's a better way to describe the region and its history: "We don't need wine terms to describe the beer revolution. It stands on its own," he says. "It should be the Garden of Eden of Craft Beer.

"Charlie Papazian served dual roles as both tempter and evangelist," Jones continues. "He offered the people the great temptation of better beer, and he served as the Moses of the movement by penning the Ten Commandments for how people could obtain that forbidden fruit and the blessings it provides," Jones says about Papazian's book, *The Joy of Homebrewing*.

"The book inspired the first wave of his disciples, who went on to open breweries and show the people a better way. Still does, of course," he concludes. "Garden of Eden remains fitting for another reason: Like Adam and Eve, men and women in Colorado live in a place that's lush with heavenly amounts of glorious beer. Seeds were sown here, and minds were blown."

10

BEER BOOM AND BUST IN THE 1990s

By the early 1990s, Colorado's economy had begun to recover from a long recession that started with the oil and gas crash in 1985 and lasted through the stock market crash of 1987 and for a few years thereafter. The telecom industry was growing quickly, and the City of Denver was investing in huge new projects like the Colorado Convention Center (1990) and Denver International Airport (1995). And developers were taking a new look at long-ignored parts of the city like the Central Platte Valley, where the iconic Elitch Gardens amusement park opened in 1995. Money poured into the state from outside developers looking to cash in on housing development and the exploding neighborhoods around Coors Field.

All of this activity made people thirsty, so these years brought a new wave of craft brewing entrepreneurs looking to make their mark in Colorado. All of them wanted to emulate the success that Hickenlooper and his partners had achieved at the Wynkoop.

A few of these startups manufactured and packaged beer only, but most were brewpubs, meaning they also served food. Prior to 1988, there had been no provision in state law that allowed a restaurant to also make and sell its own beer. But Hickenlooper's team, along with another brewery-in-planning called Denver Brewing Co., pushed the state legislature to change the law. Eventually, Colorado altered its hotel and restaurant license to allow for the concept of brewpubs. (A separate brewpub license was created in 1996). Interestingly, Denver Brewing Co., which was financed by Siebans

River North Brewery in Chicago, never actually completed its plans or opened in Lower Downtown as it had intended.

The first to follow was Frank Day, a Harvard graduate and restaurant entrepreneur who had opened the first Old Chicago in Boulder in 1976 before turning the pizza concept into a local, and then national, chain. Frank and his wife, Gina, had stepped in to rescue Boulder Beer Company when it was struggling and then opened the Walnut Brewery in Boulder in 1990. Now, the Days and partner Thomas Moxcey wanted to bring a similar brewery to Denver.

Their new idea was the Rock Bottom Restaurant and Brewery, which opened on the Sixteenth Street Mall on November 1, 1991. Nestled on the ground floor of the Prudential Building, they got the name from the Prudential insurance company, which used an image of the Rock of Gibraltar in its logo and carried the famous slogan, "Own a piece of the rock."

It was a great location, and anyone who stopped in could watch through open windows as the brewers worked—a novelty that is still fascinating to this day. In 2010, an investment firm called Centerbridge Capital Partners spent $150 million to buy a majority interest in Rock Bottom and Old Chicago, along with the Tennessee-based Gordon Biersch brewpub chain

Frank Day (*center*), shortly after helping to rescue Boulder Beer. *David Bjorkman/Brewers Association Archive.*

and other properties. The combined organization, Craftworks Restaurants and Breweries, now controls two hundred restaurants in forty states. But back then, it was a pioneer of the coming craft beer scene.

Champion Brewing Company opened in 1991 as well, boasting a huge space with pool tables, foosball, shuffleboard, big-screen TVs and a sports bar motif. Located five blocks away from Rock Bottom in historic Larimer Square, the brewery served an English-style brown, a raspberry wheat, an Irish red and a cocoa porter, among others. At lunchtime, it was a great people-watching spot, while in the evenings, customers could sit on the patio and enjoy live music.

Breckenridge Brewery, which Richard Squire founded a year earlier in the ski town of Breckenridge, opened a second location in 1991, on Blake Street cater-corner to the future site of Coors Field. Known for its Avalanche Ale, Breckenridge moved its brewing equipment to a spot on Kalamath Street in June 1996, where it continued to grow for nearly three decades until being purchased by Anheuser-Busch InBev in 2015.

Then there was Tabernash Brewing, founded by Eric Warner and Jeff Mendel in 1993 inside the historic rail-side Denargo Market. Specializing in German-style wheat beers and lagers, the brewery sold kegs to restaurants but limited its on-site sales to a seven-hundred-square-foot tasting room where it sold growlers to-go (although the staff did give out plenty of free samples).

In 1994, the Wynkoop teamed up with Flying Dog Brewing, which was founded by Aspen millionaire entrepreneur George Stranahan, a friend and neighbor of famed gonzo journalist Hunter Thompson, to create Broadway Brewing. Both companies wanted to bottle beer but neither had the resources to do it alone. Broadway pumped out flagships for both companies and turned out pizzas and calzones. It operated inside what is now the Silver State Lofts at 2441 Broadway before moving a block away to 2401 Blake Street (an address that would become home to River North Brewery nearly two decades later).

Great Divide Brewing also opened in 1994, but owner Brian Dunn didn't bother with food. Rather, he took the approach that New Belgium had taken, dedicating his entire facility to brewing and packaging beer in bottles and kegs for distribution. Like Tabernash, Great Divide offered tours and free samples for people who stopped in.

In late 1995, the short-lived Timberline Brewpub, also known as Mile High Brewing, opened at 2401 Blake Street. It closed after only a few months, however. The space was then taken over by Broadway Brewing. (Interestingly, Mile High was funded by Indian businessman Vijay Mallya

A tap handle from defunct Denver brewery Timberline found in the River North Brewery building. *Matt Hess.*

who owned several U.S. breweries in the '90s, including New York's Olde Saratoga Brewery and California's Mendocino Brewing. Mallya, now a multi-millionaire tycoon, is currently facing a slew of legal issues and criminal charges in England and India.)

Finally, Coors's Keith Villa opened The Sandlot inside Coors Field at the start of the 1995 baseball season. It was there that Villa brewed the first batches of Blue Moon Belgian Wit.

By the end of 1995, those eight breweries— plus the Wynkoop and a tenth brewery called Lonetree Brewing that was just north of the city limits— had created quite a scene.

For the legions of homebrewers who had come up on Charlie Papazian's *The Complete Joy of Homebrewing*, the smell of boiling wort and mashed grains was comforting and exciting. But for most, the novel aromas that wafted out of these breweries were thrilling and new. Champion, Rock Bottom and Wynkoop, all boasting perfect patios, were particularly packed.

And just as in 1859 when Rocky Mountain Brewery began offering what the *Rocky Mountain News* called "the best we ever tasted" in the Wild West town of Denver—and again when the Wynkoop opened in 1988—local writers and national travel guides were inflamed with passion and sometimes hyperbole. The Wynkoop named its groundbreaking Patty's Chile Beer for *Westword* founder and green chile–lover Patty Calhoun, while Champion named a beer after *Rocky Mountain News* columnist Norm Clarke. Denver Post scribe Dick Kreck, meanwhile, conducted plenty of "research" for his numerous beer stories. He was known as Mr. Beer and had the personalized license plates to prove it.

Kyle Wagner, the restaurant critic for *Westword*, took a more reserved approach when she reviewed seven of the eight breweries for a February 1995 column. Among her favorite beers were Tabernash Weiss, Rock Bottom Molly's Brown Ale and Great Divide's Saint Brigid's Porter, which she described as "a thick-tasting but light porter with a roasted chocolate flavor" and "the most sophisticated" of the brewery's beers.

The adolescent Great American Beer Festival, now in its thirteenth year, was also a source of pride for Denver residents. Held in October 1995, in the old Currigan Exhibition Hall, it attracted twenty-two thousand people who sampled 1,323 beers from 336 breweries. Some of the winners included Breckenridge Brewery's Denver Mountain Wheat and the Sandlot's Rightfield Red.

The year before, in 1994, the fledgling Tabernash Brewery had scored a big hit by winning three GABF medals for Denargo Lager, Golden Spike Lager and Tabernash Weiss. "They were making world-class wheat beers, and they were ahead of their time," says writer and publicist Marty Jones. Before moving to Denver, Jones visited in 1991 on his honeymoon. His brother-in-law, who lived here, took him to the Wynkoop—the first brewpub Jones had ever seen, and it blew his mind. So, when his wife, Lisa, suggested that they relocate from Virginia to Denver four years later, Jones agreed with the goal of getting into the beer business.

An eternal optimist with a flair for catchy phrases and down-home prose, Jones immediately went to work, looking to write a beer column. He contributed to *Celebrator*, *Empire*, *Westword* and Microsoft-owned Sidewalk.com.

Marty Jones (*left*) with famed beer writer Michael Jackson in the early 2000s. *Marty Jones.*

"People were wide eyed dreamers and beer geeks and they wanted to make good beer. For me, coming from a town with no beer culture, it was awesome," he wrote. But Jones, who was a homebrewer at the time, stopped brewing beer himself. "I lived a couple blocks from Tabernash. They would fill a growler of beer for a couple of bucks, and I could stand there and talk to the owner. It was so good, I thought, why am I even bothering to brew myself?" After all, the head brewer and cofounder, Eric Warner, "literally wrote the book on German-style wheat beers (simply called *German Wheat Beer*)," Jones pointed out.

Warner, who grew up in Aurora, Colorado, is now the brewmaster and cofounder of Karbach Brewing in Houston (now owned by Anheuser-Busch InBev), Texas, but almost no one who talks about Denver breweries in the '90s does so without mentioning his name. A 1996 graduate of Lewis and Clark College in Oregon, Warner spent a year abroad in Germany and loved it. He'd also gotten to know the Widmer and Bridgeport breweries, which were just getting started in Oregon. So, to "put off getting a real job for a while," Warner moved to Munich for three years, where he got a degree as a brewmaster from the Technische Universität München, Weihenstephan.

When he returned to Colorado, Warner, who had also interned with Russell Schehrer at the Wynkoop, did some brewery consulting work and wrote his book. But his real goal was to start his own brewery. So, in 1993, Warner, Jeff Mendel and two others opened up Tabernash Brewing.

Since everyone else at the time was brewing English or Belgian-style ales, they decided to focus on Warner's strength, German styles. It was a smart choice. By 1994, their beers had won several awards and were on tap at many bars and restaurants around town. The next year, they began transporting beer to Fort Collins where New Belgium bottled it for them.

It was an amazing time not just for Tabernash but also for all of the breweries and their employees, who found a camaraderie that pitted them against the world and drew them closer as friends rather than making them into competitors.

Great Divide, Breckenridge Brewery and Blue Moon, for instance, shared a $20,000 piece of bottling equipment, while the Wynkoop teamed up with other breweries and restaurants to buy supplies like pint glasses. "Everybody knew everybody back then," says Great Divide's Brian Dunn. "We went swimming together. We had parties together."

"There was a carefree spirit, an intimacy that you don't have today," Warner adds. "I like to think of it as being a little like Rock 'n Roll. All the bands in the late '60s knew each other and you could gig with anyone." One

Tabernash Brewing founder Eric Warner was an early winner at GABF. *David Bjorkman/Brewers Association Archive.*

of Warner's favorite memories is the grand opening party that Broadway Brewing held in the old Silver State Laundry building. At the end of the evening, staff from several breweries climbed onto a rooftop balcony to hit golf balls into the night—perhaps celebrating the risks they had taken and the long shots they had been.

But the fun didn't last long. In 1997, the bubble burst—or hit a wall, anyway. Brewery growth, which had been steaming along at more than 50 percent annually, had dropped off significantly in 1996 and then fell to just 2 percent in 1997, where it remained for more than a decade. Microbreweries in towns across Colorado began closing. The number dropped from 112 to 105 in just twelve months. And the total number of breweries nationwide leveled off at between 1,400 and 1,500, where it would stay until the brewery resurgence in 2007.

While many of the early brewery owners were driven by passion, some got into the business because they thought it would be a quick moneymaker. But brewing isn't a quick-buck business—something Papazian has pointed out many times. It's one that requires careful attention to quality, a lot of physical labor and an understanding of how to manage employees, build brands and prepare for changing commodity prices.

"A lot of these early entrepreneurs didn't have any business experience. Some of them had quality and brand issues, or distribution problems," Papazian says. "People were counting on quick growth to cover their investments. That didn't happen."

Warner was one of the passionate ones. When demand slipped, he and Mendel considered going back to their original investors to ask for more money, but those folks had lost their appetite for the market. Left Hand Brewing, which was founded in Longmont in 1993, was in the same boat. "We were all young guys without a lot of business experience, and we were both struggling. So, we decided to merge the two breweries. Left Hand had a great portfolio of beer, and so did we," Warner says.

Tabernash merged with Left Hand in 1997, and although Left Hand continued to produce Tabernash's beers for a few years, the brewery eventually discontinued them.

Champion and Lonetree (not to be confused with the currently thriving Lone Tree Brewing) both closed their doors within a few years, joining Timberline and Tabernash in the history books. John Hickenlooper, meanwhile, had invested in so many brewpubs out of state and was in a little over his head. The Wynkoop divested itself of those properties, as well as its interest in Broadway Brewing, which was subsequently renamed Flying Dog.

That's where Warner found himself working after closing Tabernash. Over the next few years, he brewed and managed Flying Dog, which stopped serving food in 2002 and leased some of its space to the Blake Street Tavern. Warner eventually left Flying Dog when the brewery moved to Frederick, Maryland, in 2008. (Three years later, River North Brewery would move into Flying Dog's old building on Blake Street, continuing its brewing legacy. The building was torn down in 2016.)

At the time, no one knew or understood that they could have legally run their breweries as taprooms without serving food or even packaging. It wouldn't be until 2005 that Kevin DeLange at Aurora's Dry Dock Brewing figured out that bit of magic.

"We kick ourselves now. We could have sold beer by the pint at Tabernash, but we didn't dig deep enough," Warner says. "If we had it to do over again, we should have figured out a way to stick it out longer. Had we survived the next couple years, we would have been in a good position to be one of the biggest craft breweries in Colorado. But at the time, no one knew the potential of how much craft beer you could sell."

II

GREAT DIVIDE BREWING'S BOLD CHARACTERS

When the microbrew market fell through the floor in 1997, Great Divide Brewing was only three years old and hardly in a position to weather the storm. Located in a former dairy building in an industrial neighborhood, it was surrounded by vacant lots and empty warehouses. Homeless people slept on the street out front and in the alley behind. Local bands used part of the space to practice at night. A snowplow company parked its vehicles there.

Founded by Brian Dunn and then-wife Tara, the brewery was the only one in Denver that wasn't attached to or associated with a restaurant. Instead, it opened by selling kegs to bars and restaurants and twenty-two-ounce bomber bottles and half-gallon jugs out the front door—a door made of steel and with no windows. Things started slowly, with just two beers that Dunn had developed in his kitchen at home, Arapahoe Amber and Whitewater Wheat.

Still, people found their way in, standing around in the taproom, which also served as the employee breakroom, and tentatively asking for tours—not that there was much to see.

Dunn didn't have time to worry about marketing, though. He was too busy keeping things afloat. While a few breweries went under or sold in 1997 and 1998, Dunn kept his head down. He'd borrowed money from friends and family to start the business and he refused to disappoint them. "It was my life," he says. "And I had a willingness and a hardheadedness to make sure it didn't fail." The head brewer for the first two or three years, Dunn would come in at three o'clock in the morning to make beer before doing paperwork, opening the taproom and then heading out to sell. He worked festivals, managed accounts, cleaned the toilets and asked homeless people to move on.

The reason? Passion.

Dunn grew up in the 1960s and '70s in Vermont in a home where eating and drinking were important. There were five kids, and his mom cooked all the time. His father liked good beer, wine and spirits, and he'd enjoy them all during big family meals. "He didn't like Bud, Miller and Coors," Dunn says. "He liked imports, so that's what he always drank."

So, when Dunn grew up and went to college at Colorado State University, that's what he looked for, too, eventually landing a job at an Old Chicago location in Fort Collins—one of the only restaurants at the time that offered imports and other interesting beers.

After graduating in 1985, Dunn headed overseas and spent five years developing farms in third-world countries, primarily in North Africa. One of his jobs was to buy groceries, so he would take a Range Rover on the ferry to France, where he'd load it up with butter, cheese, coffee, pork and, of course, beer—lots of beer—from Belgium, France and Germany. After his time in Africa, Dunn started traveling throughout Europe and Asia, drinking new beers in every country. "I got really into it," he says. "By the time I came back to the United States, I'd been to forty countries."

Back in Denver, he began hanging out at the Wynkoop and homebrewing enthusiastically, joining a now legendary homebrew club called the Unfermentables. Other members included Wynkoop's Russell Shearer and Wayne Waananen, the first brewer at the Sandlot inside Coors Field.

Dunn also enrolled at Univeristy of Denver, where he earned a master's degree in environmental policy and management and began looking for jobs. One of his potential employers was in Fresno, California, but as he sat on the plane, he thought to himself, "I don't want this job. What the fuck am I doing?" On the plane ride back, he wrote a business plan for a brewery. Like so many others in the brewing industry who came before and after him, Dunn decided to follow his passion instead of continuing on his previously chosen career path.

It was late 1992, and Dunn, hilariously in retrospect, thought he was late to the game. After all, Wynkoop and Breckenridge Brewery were up and running, as was Rock Bottom and Champion. How many breweries could Denver support? But as he surveyed dozens of liquor stores and bars in the vicinity, he kept getting the same answer: "If your beer is good, we'll buy it."

Dunn found what would become the Great Divide building by searching the classified ads in the *Denver Post* and signed a lease for five thousand square feet. Originally built for dairy uses, the structure had the bones he needed—floor drains, thick walls, access to lots of power and water.

After a series of zoning and construction hurdles, Dunn was finally ready to brew in early May 1993—in time, he hoped, to have a beer in the upcoming Colorado Brewers Festival in Fort Collins, which, in its third year, was second only to GABF in terms of importance. The festival also happened to be the same weekend of his wedding.

Unfortunately, the first brew day took a tragic turn when the man who Dunn had hired to help out died in a car accident on his way to Denver. Dunn didn't find out what had happened to him until later, so in the interim, he relied on the experience of John Legnard, a brewer at the year-old H.C. Berger Brewing in Fort Collins, who he hired to help convert his five-gallon homebrew recipes onto his new seventeen-barrel system. Dunn had met Legnard months earlier when he'd volunteered at H.C. Berger to gain experience. (Shortly thereafter, the Sandlot's Wayne Waananen hired Legnard; Legnard went on to help grow Blue Moon and the Denver beer scene in general. He eventually took over as head of the new Blue Moon pub in River North, where he still is.)

Great Divide founder Brian Dunn with his original brewhouse in the early 1990s. *David Bjorkman/Brewers Association Archive.*

But Dunn needed a new brewer, and before he could start asking around, someone from Breckenridge Brewery read the story about the accident and dropped by with a folder full of resumes. "That was the first time I was really introduced to the openness and sharing that are a part of this industry," Dunn says. It was also the start of a close relationship.

Breckenridge, founded in the ski town of the same name, opened its Denver location just four blocks away in 1991 and was turning out beers like Avalanche Ale, Mountain Wheat and Oatmeal Stout. (It also famously brewed Popus Visitus Welcome Ale in honor of Pope John Paul II's visit to Denver in 1993. The label on the twenty-two-ounce bomber bottle depicted stained glass in the background and a sendup of the hands of God and Adam nearly touching in Michelangelo's *The Creation of Adam*—but with God's hand holding a foamy beer.)

Though the brewery was not new to the scene, it was small and there were some days when management would show up and not be sure if they'd be able to open the doors, says Todd Thibault, who joined Breckenridge in 1994. "We didn't have a lot of money, and sometimes we couldn't pay for something, so we'd borrow stuff back and forth all the time." If Great Divide didn't have a gasket, Dunn could get one from Breckenridge. If Breckenridge ran out of bottle caps, head brewer Todd Usry would borrow some from Great Divide. The breweries even shared a bottle filler and a forklift, which they'd drive back and forth along what was then a mostly empty Twenty-Second Street.

The two breweries grew quickly, and while Breckenridge focused on its pub business, Great Divide continued to take up more space for manufacturing, adding another two thousand square feet and then another three thousand. Eventually, the brewery kicked out the building's other tenants and shifted the practicing bands into whatever space it could find for them.

Local beer writer and microbrew evangelist Marty Jones was in one of those bands. "We rehearsed there in the old yogurt room because it had two-foot-thick walls," he says. "As the brewery grew, we moved upstairs and all around." But Jones, who had a knack for catchy lyrics, realized he also had some creative ideas for how to help Great Divide with its marketing.

So, Dunn, who'd come to realize that the company needed a tagline, hired Jones, "for not much money," Dunn says, to write one. That line, "great minds drink alike," is still used by the brewery in much of its advertising and branding. Over the next two years, Jones also wrote press releases, copy for bottle labels and plenty of other marketing material and slogans.

Jones later did the same for New Belgium, where he wrote the slogan "contents under pressure"; Oskar Blues, where he helped fashion "the canned beer apocalypse"; and Wynkoop Brewing, where he helped create a memorable beer made from bull testicles, or Rocky Mountain oysters, as they are euphemistically called. He also did press work for the Colorado Brewers Guild, the BA and numerous festivals, including GABF.

By the year 2000, Great Divide was doing well enough to buy its building, expand its capacity and distribute to other states, and by 2005, the brewery had earned a reputation for pushing the envelope with big, bold, highly rated beers like Hercules Double IPA and Yeti Imperial Stout. These beers stood out in part because the rest of Denver's craft beer scene had stagnated since the slowdown of 1997 when several breweries closed. In fact, aside from one or two startups like Pints Pub, which began making its own English-style cask ales in 1996, and Heavenly Daze, which operated in Denver in 1998 and 1999, everything was exactly the same.

It would remain that way until 2010 when Strange Craft Beer Company opened, kicking off a new wave of brewery openings and starting the current taproom culture.

That movement caught Great Divide a little off guard. While the brewery had expanded its taproom slightly, it was still pouring free tasters, like New Belgium and some of the other old-school beermakers. In fact, Great Divide didn't start charging for pints in its small taproom until 2012, though it began donating all of the proceeds to charity.

The growth of craft beer culture was great for the bottom line, however. In fact, demand for Great Divide's beers was so strong that Dunn realized he was going to need to find a second location. In 2013, he began quietly assembling land along Brighton Boulevard in the River North Arts District about a mile away, eventually buying five acres for $9 million.

In 2014, he unveiled plans for a $38 million brewing campus. The first phase called for a sixty-five-thousand-square-foot warehouse, storage and packaging facility, and a taproom called the Barrel Bar. The second phase was to include a new brewhouse capable of producing 250,000 barrels of beer per year, along with a taproom, restaurant and beer garden.

Construction on the first phase finished in mid-2015, but the market began experiencing a second slowdown soon after, and Great Divide suffered a 16 percent production decline in 2016. It was the first time in the brewery's history that it had made less beer than in the previous year. But Great Divide revamped its lineup the following year and began adapting to change. In 2019, it canceled plans for the second phase of

Denver's iconic Great Divide Brewing built a second location in 2014. *Jonathan Shikes.*

construction and sold off its excess land. The brewery is now poised for significant growth if the market recovers.

"Today's scene is awesome," Dunn says. "Ten to fifteen years ago, Denver was very behind. We just weren't very impressive compared to places like Seattle, Portland, New York and Chicago. But things got better, styles opened up and the brewers became more experienced." Some of those brewers earned their chops at Great Divide, which has been a training ground for nearly a dozen brewers who went on to start their own places.

12

ONCE IN A BLUE MOON

Bill Coors stood along one side of the L-shaped bar on the sixth floor of the massive Coors complex in Golden. The company's leadership met there once a day to talk. He ordered a Coors (original). The executives who reported directly to him stood nearby, each drinking a Coors as well. Bill's nephew Pete Coors and his direct reports stood along the other leg of the L. Each had a Coors Light in hand. Keith Villa was behind the bar, and he'd presented these lager men with an abomination: a cloudy ale smelling of oranges and coriander.

"They didn't care for the taste or the smell or the look of it," Villa says about that day in 1994. Though Villa didn't know then that the beer would change the industry, he knew it was great. "I promised myself right then and there that I would make it a success."

Down the road in Denver, the beer was already being brewed in the basement of Coors Field under the codename Bellyslide Belgian White and was being served to tens of thousands of Colorado Rockies fans who were turning out in droves to see their two-year-old Major League Baseball team play in the beautiful new ballpark. By the end of the baseball season, the beer was a bestseller.

More than twenty-five years later, Blue Moon Belgian White is distributed in all fifty states and twenty-five countries and is the number-one selling beer in the "craft" segment in the United States. But it took a lot of work and a lot of ingenuity. And it took Villa to lead the way.

A pennant advertising the original Belly Slide Belgian Wit. *Blue Moon Brewing.*

A second-generation Colorado native, Villa took an unusual path to his job at Coors. The son of a nurse and a construction foreman, he grew up in Wheat Ridge, Colorado, just a few miles from Golden, and went to Pomona High School, where he was one of the only Latinos in his class. After that, he took off for the University of Colorado to study science.

One day in 1982, during his freshman year at CU, Villa ran into some people on the Pearl Street Mall who were handing out flyers about a homebrewing class. Homebrewing had been legalized nationwide just four years earlier, and Boulder had become a major player in the scene thanks to enigmatic beer visionary and homebrewing champion Charlie Papazian.

Villa took up the hobby while pursuing a degree in molecular biology. In 1986, as he was getting ready to graduate with plans to go to medical school to be a pediatrician, Villa saw a job ad for a brewing scientist that Coors had posted on campus. He applied and after a few days was told that he was the most qualified applicant and could start work after graduation. (Villa, like many Coors employees before him, had to take a controversial lie detector test before being hired. The company put the policy in place after Adolph Coors III was kidnapped and murdered in 1960. The company was eventually forced to do away with the policy.)

It was a change of plans, but Villa figured he'd take the job, and if he didn't like it, medical school was waiting for him. But he did like it. In fact, Coors sent their promising scientist to Brussels, Belgium, to learn more at Vrije Universiteit Brussel. Villa stayed in Europe from 1988 to 1992, earning his PhD, traveling and learning about abbey ales, witbiers, sours and saisons.

"Back then, Belgium was a hidden jewel, not a tourist draw," he says. "And while I was there, I learned about all the ways they made their crazy beers. What a lot of people don't realize is that the Belgians rarely brew to style guidelines. They brew to taste." It was a notion he took back to the states and one he had in his head in 1994, when Coors asked the young scientist to help direct two unusual projects.

The first project was to research and develop a new drinkable, full-flavored beer that Coors could package and add to its small lineup of specialty microbrews, like George Killian's Irish Red, an amber lager, and Winterfest, a seasonal beer. "Killian's was the number one craft brand back then," Villa says. "It was a very small market." But thanks to the success of the first wave of craft breweries, like New Belgium and Odell, drinkers were looking for new flavors.

Keith Villa created Blue Moon Brewing and ran it for more than two decades. *Blue Moon Brewing.*

The second project was to research breweries and brewpubs across the country to create a similar operation inside Coors Field. Coors, which held an ownership stake in the young team, had also bought the naming rights to the then-under-construction ballpark, and as part of its marketing strategy, the company planned to put a small brewery inside a historic brick warehouse building that was being incorporated into the stadium's design.

So, Villa, along with fellow Coors brewer Dave Bright and engineer Mike Medford, traveled the country exploring as many brewpubs as they could. These included some early brewpub pioneers in Colorado, like the Champion, Rock Bottom and Wynkoop breweries in Denver; HC Berger in Fort Collins; and the Oasis and Walnut breweries in Boulder. These were the breweries that kicked off the first wave of microbrews in Colorado.

But at nearly every visit, people cautioned the Coors team against visiting one Boulder brewpub in particular: Mountain Sun. "They all said, 'Don't go to Mountain Sun. They are crazy and they don't brew to style,'" Villa recalls. "So, of course we went. It was the last one."

There they met head brewer Jack Harris, who had come to Boulder with Mountain Sun cofounder Kevin Daly. Daly had gone to law school in Portland and came to love microbrews while he hung out at one of the early McMenamins breweries, where Harris was working. Harris would go on to work at many other breweries, eventually founding Fort George Brewery and Public House in Astoria, Oregon, but he was perfecting his style—or lack thereof—in Boulder. "He really stuck out," Villa says. "His business card had about twenty titles on it." They included jester, window cleaner, cook, skateboard technician and, Harris's personal favorite, bon vivant.

"And he brewed to taste rather than to style," Villa adds, just like the Belgians. "It was awesome, and I thought, 'This is how we should build out the Sandlot at Coors Field.'"

Coors Field opened in April 1995, and the Sandlot (then known as Rounders) followed in September. It was the first—and still just one of two—breweries inside a Major League ballpark. Today, the Sandlot (now called Blue Moon Brewing at the Sandlot) still operates on a small but beautiful copper-plated brewing system in the basement of the building. It turns out dozens of beers per year, mostly German-style lagers, and has won at least forty-five medals at the Great American Beer Festival—more than any other brewery in Colorado.

Villa hired Wayne Waananen as the first head brewer. Waananen, who had started a homebrewing club years earlier with the Wynkoop's Russell Shearer, was working at Hubcap Brewing (now defunct) in Vail. Although the recipe was envisioned and developed by Villa, Waananen was the first to actually brew a batch of it, in the basement brewery.

On opening day in April 1995, Bellyslide Belgian White went on tap, along with Squeeze Play Wheat, Power Alley ESB, Rightfield Red Ale, Slugger Stout and Pinch Hit Pilsner.

Though it was based on the traditional Belgian wits that Villa enjoyed in Belgium, this beer was brewed with a different kind of yeast, and it had the sweeter Valencia orange peel rather than the Curaçao orange peel, which is more bitter, along with coriander. Light and easy to drink, it boasted a smooth mouthfeel from oats and a cloudy appearance.

That last part took people by surprise. Hazy and unfiltered, it resembled juice more than beer. "I thought it would be a huge hit. But people thought something was wrong with it," Villa says. "I thought it was a work of art myself. But people had to be convinced."

Things weren't going so well at Coors headquarters either. The brewing staff refused to let Villa make Blue Moon on the industrial system for fear that the Belgian yeast would infect or contaminate the ingredients. So, Villa took the beer to a handful of different contract brewers, mostly in the eastern United States, who agreed to brew it. He officially introduced it as Blue Moon Belgian White at the Sandlot in September 1995.

The brand grew slowly—very slowly—in the first few years. "Pete Coors admits publicly that he tried to kill it three times. I would say four," Villa laughs. (Pete Coors himself acknowledges this.)

So, Villa decided to launch a low-budget marketing campaign, hosting educational beer dinners and touring the country teaching bartenders and drinkers about the style. He also added the signature orange slice that is now commonly served with Blue Moon—something that turned out to be a challenge. Bars wanted to serve it with a lemon because they had them around for other drinks, but no one had oranges. So, Villa brought them bags of oranges and showed them how to cut them just right so the slices wouldn't flop to one side.

Eventually, the bars started catching on, especially when customers started demanding their oranges. "Sales would take off, tips went up," he says. In 1998, Villa got the idea to add a unique glass to complete the unusual presentation. "I did everything I could to keep it alive. It only grew by single digits in the first few years." But by 2002, Blue Moon reached critical mass and began to grow steadily for the next fifteen years. Today, there are dozens of Blue Moon flavors, many of which got their start at the Sandlot.

By 2017, the brand had become such a hit—it did sales of $258 million in grocery and convenience stores in 2017—that Coors agreed to open a huge, expensive brewpub in Denver's densest brewery neighborhood, the River North Arts District, home to at least a dozen other breweries. Though

The Sandlot opened inside Coors Field in 1995. *Jonathan Shikes.*

Waananen left Blue Moon after two years—he worked most recently as the head brewer for Station 26 Brewing in Denver—he had hired Tom Hail and John Legnard (the same John Legnard who'd helped Brian Dunn brew his very first batch of beer at Great Divide) to run the place. Hail now manages the Sandlot, and Legnard oversees the Blue Moon brewpub.

Pete Coors and the rest of the staff at the company's now-closed headquarters in downtown Denver took a lot of meetings there. "Early on, they gave us the funds, but not a lot of support. Now, it is different," Villa says. "Pete saw this coming, and he has the capacity to change." In fact, although Pete Coors still prefers Coors Light, he'll try just about anything—from a Belgian gueuze to a German bock. And, yes, he now loves Blue Moon.

Villa stepped down from Coors at the very beginning of 2018 and shortly thereafter announced that he would create a new company, Ceria, selling non-alcoholic beer infused with THC, the psychoactive ingredient in marijuana. The first beer he made? A Belgian-style wit with orange and coriander.

13

NO CRAP ON TAP

It was a Thursday night in September 1997, and Chris Black was treading the dirty red carpet inside Denver's long-since demolished Currigan Hall, telling brewers and beer drinkers at the sixteenth annual Great American Beer Festival about his four-month-old beer bar, the Falling Rock Tap House. Black and his brother, Steve, had moved from Houston to Denver just a year earlier to open the bar, which had sixty-nine different handles of "no crap on tap," in part because of GABF—a Mecca for people who like all kinds of beer.

Black had spent a couple of hours walking up and down the rows of beer booths, handing out about one thousand cards that promised fifty cents off of a beer, when he got a call on his big flip phone at around 9:00 p.m. It was Steve: "Stop handing out cards and get back here," he told Chris, a little panic in his voice. The place was slammed. When he got to Falling Rock—located about a block from Coors Field—there was a line out the door. "I jumped behind the bar and started pouring beers as fast as I could," he says.

That line was nothing compared to what Falling Rock would get over the next two decades, though, as it grew into Denver's biggest and best-known craft beer bar—on par with some of the nation's most famous, like The Toronado in San Francisco, Hopleaf in Chicago and Monk's Cafe in Philadelphia. During the Great American Beer Festival in 2019, Falling Rock held more than thirty different events over seven days, starting with the annual GABF week kickoff complete with a digital countdown clock on

Charlie Papazian and Chris Black were both BA board members. *Photo by Michael Meyers for the Brewers Association.*

Monday and ending with a traditional tapping of beers from New Belgium Brewing on Saturday night.

"Prior to us opening, people's idea of what to do with GABF was to hang a sign out front that said, 'Buckets of Sam Adams for 10 bucks,'" Black says. "There were mobs of people running around town, and all they could find was the same old shit. Most of them were shocked." There were a few breweries, like Wynkoop, Breckenridge and Great Divide, as well as a handful of haunts, like My Brothers Bar, the Cherry Cricket and Old Chicago, that carried craft, but for the most part, the city was missing an opportunity to capitalize on what was becoming the biggest beer festival of its kind in the world.

The lack of good beer was one of the things that put Denver on the radar for the Black brothers. They knew they could fix it.

Chris Black grew up in Texas, the son of an Exxon corporate attorney, and got into the beer business in the early 1980s, working for importers, distributors and a few early microbreweries. His brother, Steve, worked at the Ginger Man, a string of beer bars that started in Houston in 1985. Once a year, Black would take a business trip to Denver, but he quickly learned that most bars only featured Miller, Coors, Bud and other light lagers. It was even hard to find a Paulaner, which was one of the brands Black sold. The more he thought about it, the more he figured that Denver would be a perfect place for something like the Ginger Man. "I put that in the back of my head," he says.

Then, in the mid-1990s, Black's dad told his sons that he was getting ready to retire and wanted to do something with his money. More than that, he wanted his sons to strike out on their own. He wasn't expecting them to do it Denver, but he came around after touring the city. The Blacks began looking for a spot near Coors Field, which had just been built in the newly burgeoning LoDo neighborhood. They found a good one—a former receiving dock for an electrical supply company at 1919 Blake Street that was just yards away from home plate. Black loved the way it was set back from the street, giving the place a patio and an indoor/outdoor feel. The landlord loved the fact that Falling Rock would be something other than a-shot-and-a-beer place.

Falling Rock's GABF countdown clock hits zero. *Jonathan Shikes.*

Falling Rock opened in June 1997 with sixty different beers on sixty-nine taps—none of them Miller, Bud or Coors. Black did have Coors in bottles, but the amount he sells today has dropped to almost nothing. "We would do ten to fifteen cases of industrial lager during baseball games," Black says. "Now, if we do three or four, it's a big week for them."

The name of the bar comes from the ubiquitous diamond-shaped yellow warning signs that dot Colorado's mountain highways. "My wife and I were driving up Berthoud pass and we kept seeing the signs every hundred yards," Black recalls. "I jokingly said, 'Why don't we just call it Falling Rock and let the Department of Transportation do our advertising for us.' We played around with it, and we never came up with another name after that."

And Falling Rock grew as LoDo grew, developing a split personality as a hot party bar in this baseball neighborhood but also as a destination for beer geeks—not just from Colorado, but also from the rest of the country and around the world.

That dual role may also be why Falling Rock has developed a reputation over the years for a somewhat curmudgeonly staff—something Black embraces as an extension of his and his brother's personalities. "We're not Applebee's. We don't have front-door greeters and we don't have a corporate script," he laughs. Most of his employees have worked in the industry for a while, and most know a lot about beer.

"If you get asked the same stupid questions a thousand times a day, it grinds on you. We answer questions simply, without flowery language. We are not trying to be rude, but we're busy and we are trying to get the information to you as quickly as possible and get on to the next person."

That didn't stop people from pouring in the doors. For years, Falling Rock was the only place in Denver where breweries from other Colorado towns could put their beers on tap. New Belgium, Ska, Oskar Blues, Left Hand and Odell all relied on Chris Black. But Black didn't just showcase the state. He also sought up-and-coming breweries from out of state, including Stone, Dogfish Head, Russian River, Victory, Lost Abbey and Maui Brewing, many of which have gone on to become the largest, most important craft breweries in the country. Those early connections helped Colorado develop as a state where breweries wanted to send their newest beers.

Falling Rock now has close to ninety beers on tap and hundreds of bottles in its cellars, and Black can be credited for almost single-handedly pushing craft beer into the spotlight in Denver and creating an entire beer culture that didn't exist before.

Chris Black founded the Falling Rock Taphouse with "no crap on tap." *Jonathan Shikes.*

New Belgium Brewing's Kim Jordan believes Black was fundamental in creating Denver's craft scene. Aside from Old Chicago and the Cherry Cricket, there weren't very many places in the city where she could sell beer. "We needed all of them back then. We needed someone to carry the flag. And although Old Chicago was great, they were a chain, she points out. "You didn't know people there the way you could know Chris at Falling Rock," she says.

Black also helped speed along the notion that people could go to a beer bar and have "a more intimate" experience with a brewery. By highlighting different breweries on different nights or tapping kegs of beer that weren't readily available somewhere else, beer fans could learn something new every time they went.

Falling Rock finally got some competition in the early 2010s when a handful of other craft beer bars, including Freshcraft, Star Bar, Euclid Hall and Hops & Pie, opened in town. Since then, dozens of others have followed suit. For the most part, Black doesn't mind the competition, and he often advises new craft beer bar owners.

But Black still rules the roost. In fact, he calls himself "the king," a king who is known by some as a tyrant and by others as a loving monarch. In the former category are some of the breweries that Black has tangled with. One of those is Oskar Blues, which got on Black's bad side by opening its own competing craft beer bar in downtown Denver, something he saw as betrayal by a company he helped build up. Another is Breckenridge Brewery, one of Colorado's oldest craft breweries, which was purchased by Anheuser-Busch InBev, the maker of Budweiser, in 2015. Black, like many other craft specialists in town, has decided not to serve beer from the industrial giant because he feels like AB InBev uses its leverage to hurt smaller breweries.

In the category of those who see Black as a loving monarch are many young breweries that are looking to get their name out there. A handle at Falling Rock means the world to them, and Black enjoys searching for great new beers and putting them on tap. He also attends many new brewery openings and events, searching out new beers for his bar.

"It's kind of overwhelming and very time consuming," he says about the number of new breweries that vie for his attention. "I used to have to drive thirty or sixty miles to get unusual beers, beers you couldn't find. Now they come mostly to me. The number one thing I'm looking for is something that fills a niche on the wall, something I don't have represented. I don't want to put on another normal IPA if it isn't going to stand out."

More often than not, he is disappointed by the beers he sees. Some are poorly made or have obvious off flavors or flaws. But others take him totally by surprise, and it's those moments that make him smile. One example is Sad Panda, a coffee stout from a little Fort Collins brewery called Horse & Dragon Brewing. "Who would have thought a coffee porter? But it's a great beer and I sell a keg a week. With ninety beers on tap now, they sell a keg a week. That's great. They are killing it."

14

THE CANNED BEER APOCALYPSE

Like a lot of brewers in 2002, Dave Thibodeau was minding his own business, happily kegging and bottling his beer when he got an unsolicited call from Kersten Kloss, a salesman at Cask Brewing Systems (now called Cask Global Canning Solutions), a small manufacturing company in Calgary, Canada. Cask had a dumb idea. They wanted to sell microbreweries on the idea of canning their beers. It would be cheaper and lighter, and it would protect their beer from the sun better than bottles.

Cans, of course, had been around since 1935 when the first steel beer cans were introduced shortly after Prohibition. Nearly thirty years later, Coors Brewing, and Bill Coors in particular, invented the seamless aluminum can, which quickly caught on because it was lighter and more sterile than steel. It also had value, like glass, for people who recycled, helping with a public relations problem that beer and soda companies were dealing with as the landscape had become cluttered with litter, primarily cans.

But by the 1980s, cans were associated with cheap, light lagers—the very beers that microbreweries had come into existence to almost entirely reject. A lot of people thought canned beers tasted like tin foil, which didn't hurt light lagers so much but didn't seem appropriate with tastier, more flavorful microbrews. So, canning a good beer seemed laughable. Cans weren't respectable. They were inferior.

Thibodeau and his Ska Brewing cofounder Bill Graham didn't mind bad ideas, though, so they listened longer than most of the other breweries Cask had talked to. "[Kersten] really liked ska music and he had this idea

Ska Brewing owners Bill Graham (*left*), Dave Thibodeau (*top*) and Matt Vincent. *Ska Brewing.*

for a black and white checkered can. It really got our wheels turning," Thibodeau says. The biggest problem was that Ska, which is located in the southern Colorado town of Durango, had just invested in a new bottling line and didn't want to cannibalize its own sales or deal with any new packaging headaches.

Up north, in the town of Lyons, Dale Katechis, who had opened Oskar Blues Grill and Brew in 1997, received a fax from Kloss with a similar sales pitch. Katechis laughed too. But since his restaurant was in a tiny town, Katechis was always looking for gimmicks that would attract attention and bring in customers from Boulder and other surrounding cities and towns. He decided to fly to Canada and meet with Cask founder Peter Love.

The visit changed his mind, and Katechis returned to Lyons with a tiny tabletop canning machine that could handle just two cans at the time. Then he turned to marketing guru Marty Jones, who had worked with Great Divide, New Belgium and others, and together they created a marketing campaign that embraced the negative attitudes toward aluminum and twisted them around. They called it "the canned beer apocalypse."

Ska Brewing, meanwhile, had turned down Cask, but as soon as Thibodeau and Graham heard that Katechis was planning to can Dale's Pale Ale, they thought, "Damn! Why didn't we pull the trigger on that?" Ska bought a canning machine as well. "I wish we would have had the balls to do it first," Thibodeau says with his characteristic deprecating sense of humor. "But I'm super glad it was them. We only put one beer into cans for the first ten years, our ESB, so we never would have made it into a thing. But Marty is fun and too good at being smart and funny and getting the word out. Cans really sent Oskar Blues on their way."

Today, canned beer is the fastest-growing segment in the craft industry. Though bottles still dominate, the volume of cans grew from 13 percent of the market by volume in 2013 to 25 percent in 2017, according to Broomfield-based Ball Corporation, the world's largest maker of aluminum cans. Sales in stores reached $932 million in 2017, double what they had been in 2015, according to data compiled by IRA, a big data firm that tracks retail sales. And those numbers, which are gathered from scans, don't take into account how much canned beer is being sold directly out of the doors of breweries themselves.

Perusing the aisles of any store in Colorado that sells craft beer, it's hard to imagine that just ten years ago—even five years ago—canning was still the industry's ugly stepchild. There are hundreds of options in four-packs,

Dale Katechis of Oskar Blues with his first canning machine. *Oskar Blues.*

Colorado cans come in all shapes and sizes. *Jonathan Shikes.*

six-packs and twelve-packs. There are 12.0-ounce, 16.0-ounce and even 19.2-ounce cans, not to mention crowlers, which are 32.0-ounce cans that can be filled at the taproom and sold in liquor stores. Some come from the tiniest breweries in the state that hire a mobile canner or a contract brewer to package the beers. Others are from breweries—both small, medium and large—that invested in their own canning lines. Many are from the largest beermakers in the state.

Oskar Blues has since become one of the two largest craft breweries in Colorado, where it also operates seven restaurants and a coffeeshop. It also has two large breweries in North Carolina and Texas. In 2015, with financial backing from a private investment firm, Oskar Blues began buying other craft breweries with similar mindsets. Today, that group, known fittingly as Canarchy, is the eighth-largest craft beer company in the nation.

But things started small. Born and raised in Alabama, Katechis understood restaurants early on—his grandfather founded Chris' Hot Dogs, a Montgomery, Alabama institution. In college at Auburn University, Katechis started homebrewing in his bathtub with a kit he'd gotten for Christmas. After graduating and marrying his high school sweetheart, Christi, Katechis decided to move west, landing in Boulder in 1992.

By then, the homebrewing movement that Charlie Papazian had started in 1978 was going strong, and Katechis, who got a job at Old Chicago Pizza and Taproom, fit right in. He joined Hop Barley and the Alers, a legendary homebrew club, and hung out at What's Brewin' Homebrew Supply, where he met guys like Eric Wallace, Gordon Knight, Adam Avery and Kevin Daly. All four had come up through the homebrewing ranks and in the next year would start Left Hand Brewing, High Country Brewery, Avery Brewing and Mountain Sun, respectively. The owner of What's Brewin', Paul Gatza, later got a job with Papazian's Brewers Association, where he now serves as the organization's director.

In April 1997, Katechis decided to follow in his family's footsteps, opening a restaurant and serving the southern dishes he'd grown up eating. But the location he picked in Lyons was a little bit sleepy. Located sixteen miles north of Boulder, it had just fourteen hundred residents. By 1999, he knew he'd have to change things up or Oskar Blues Grill and Brew wasn't going to survive.

Dale Katechis, seen here at GABF, built Oskar Blues from scratch. *Oskar Blues.*

The Dale's Pale Ale can has become iconic in Colorado. *Oskar Blues.*

In the years since he'd moved to Colorado, Katechis had become acutely aware of how crazy the population had gone for microbreweries. After a big boom in the early 1990s, there had been a bit of a crash in 1997. But people were still drinking tons of craft beer, and there were several dozen breweries throughout the state. Katechis decided it would be the perfect thing to bring customers into Oskar Blues. So, he bought a small brewing system from a now-defunct California brewery, refined one of his old homebrewing recipes, a 6 percent ABV Centennial-hopped pale ale, and served the beer at the bar. Dale's Pale Ale was a hit, and Katechis hired a full-time brewer to come up with more recipes to can.

"We were like kindred spirits with Dale and Marty," Dave Thibodeau remembers. "We had so many problems canning beer." There were leaky seams, carbonation trouble, half-full beers and supply problems. "We didn't have anyone else to talk to about it. We didn't have any tools to fix things, so we made them ourselves. For a while, to see if our cans were full enough, we would put two into a trash can filled with water. If they floated, they weren't full enough. So, we would pull those out and drink them ourselves."

But little by little, canning caught on. A couple dozen small breweries across the country began canning in 2004, and a year later, bigger breweries like Maui Brewing, Surly, Sly Fox and 21st Amendment joined the movement. In Colorado, Breckenridge Brewery (which borrowed a canning line from Ska), Steamworks Brewing, Wynkoop Brewing (where Marty Jones had since moved) and New Belgium Brewing all began canning in 2009. Seven Colorado breweries and twenty-seven nationwide canned or made plans to can beer that year.

Odell Brewing, one of Colorado's leaders, wasn't one of them. In 2009, Doug Odell told *Westword* that he much preferred glass. "I think it's a classier look," he said. But Odell admitted that canned beers had gained fans. "People used to associate canned beer with cheap beer. I think craft brewers are changing that." Odell began canning in 2015.

By 2012, about 150 breweries were canning upward of five hundred different beers nationwide, according to craftcans.com, a website that tracked canned craft beer. In the next five years, even the holdouts among the largest craft beer makers in the country—Sierra Nevada, Boston Beer Company, Firestone Walker and Lagunitas—succumbed as well.

Today, there are many hundreds of breweries canning thousands of beers across the country. Cask has placed more than one thousand canning lines in fifty-two countries around the world and recently donated a canning line to Metropolitan State University of Denver, where it will be overseen by Tivoli Brewing.

Cans, they all realized, were easier to take outdoors because they don't break. They were lighter to ship, fully recyclable, cheaper to produce and protected beer from light damage. They could also be just as resistant to oxygen if packaged correctly—just like Cask's Kersten Kloss told Thibodeau and Katechis all the way back in 2002.

In 2008, Ska had grown enough to build a new production plant, where it still operates today as one of Colorado's ten largest breweries. But it wouldn't have happened without cans, Thibodeau says. "They mean everything to us. If we had stuck with bottles, we never would have made that leap, we never would have grown like we did."

15

DRY DOCK AND THE CREATION OF TAPROOM CULTURE

Kevin DeLange wasn't where he wanted to be. A history major with a love for beer and hockey, DeLange and his college sweetheart, Michelle Reding, had moved to Denver after they both graduated from Iowa State University in 1998. Reding caught on immediately as a pension actuary, but Delange bounced around, finding fugitives as a skip tracer, then overseeing teachers who worked at night as an administrator at a for-profit college. But he longed for something else.

So, in 2002, he started searching the classified ads for businesses for sale. It could have been anything, really. A liquor store, maybe, since he liked beer. A pizza place like the one his dad had opened when he was in the sixth grade in Algona, Iowa. It turned out that DeLange, who had been a homebrewer since he was twenty-one, decided to buy an eight-year-old homebrew shop called the Brew Hut in the sprawling Denver suburb of Aurora, Colorado.

Homebrewing was "going nuts" at the time. Although the hobby had been growing in popularity since Charlie Papazian founded the American Homebrewing Association in 1978, it was really starting to catch on with the ability to order supplies over the internet. The Brew Hut was one of only three of four homebrew shops in the Denver area at the time, but it wasn't doing much online. DeLange figured he'd change that and move the shop from Aurora to another suburb, Arvada, where he lived.

Instead, he realized that the strong local customer base was critical and that moving the store would mean he'd have to start all over. So, he stayed, and it was one of the best decisions he could have made. For two years,

Delange operated the store by himself, increasing the inventory and growing sales by 30 percent each year. He worked on his own recipes, learned new techniques and got to know a number of professional brewers and serious homebrewers in the area. They included Rock Bottom brewmaster John Hanley; Gordon Schuck, who cofounded Funkwerks in 2010 in Fort Collins; Tim Myers, who opened Strange Craft Beer Company the same year; and Brian O'Connell, who would go on to start Renegade Brewing in 2011.

It was fun, but there was something DeLange just couldn't get out of his head. Back in 2002, the previous owner of the store, Scott Newcomb, had given him an idea. He'd told DeLange that if no one bought the shop, he had been planning to open a small brewery and sell pints across the bar. It was a crazy idea. Colorado's existing breweries operated as one of two models. Some, like Rock Bottom, Wynkoop and Breckenridge, were brewpubs, offering customers the full restaurant experience, and the rest, like New Belgium, Odell and Great Divide, specialized in manufacturing and packaging. Most of the latter gave tours that ended with free samples in "tasting" rooms where they also sold bottled beer to go.

Dry Dock Brewing founders Michelle Reding and Kevin Delange. *Dry Dock Brewing.*

None of these manufacturing breweries were selling pints over the bar, though. In fact, many people at the time figured it would have violated Colorado's complicated, post-Prohibition-era liquor laws.

DeLange, who'd grown accustomed to doing a lot of research while he was in graduate school, decided to find out. After being told "no" twice by the city, he went to the state and discovered a loophole that everyone else had overlooked. Decades earlier, when the only two breweries in the state were Coors and Anheuser-Busch (which opened its Fort Collins plant in 1982), a wholesalers license allowed them to sell beer to wholesalers that would then sell it to liquor stores, bars and restaurants, known as retailers. But the state department of revenue also allowed any company with a liquor wholesalers license to sell pints or packages directly to the public. The reason for this, says Laura Harris, who worked for the department for twenty-five years, was so that consumers who visited the breweries for tours could also buy some beer to-go in the gift shop. They could have sold pints, but that wasn't the goal.

"Those big brewers never wanted to develop a concept where they invited consumers in to drink," she says. After all, "that is what the retailers were for—and they respected that." When microbreweries came along, the department's liquor enforcement division (LED) explained the rules to them, including the part about selling beer to go, she adds; although, "it was certainly nothing we advertised."

A bigger problem may have been local zoning rules in individual towns and cities—or it may have just been an assumption on the part of small breweries that they couldn't do it. Whatever it was, DeLange was the first to call Harris, who served as the head of the LED at that point, and he came away satisfied that he was within the law.

So, DeLange and Reding leased a tiny, eight-hundred-square-foot space next to The Brew Hut and began hunting for brewing equipment. It wasn't easy. DeLange went through an issue of *Rocky Mountain Brewing News* and called every Colorado brewery he could find, asking if they had any used equipment for sale. "Some of them didn't understand why I wanted it. Others were excited. But no one had anything to sell," he says. Finally, about a week later, Ska Brewing co-owner Matt Vincent called back and suggested that DeLange talk to Tom Hennessey, a longtime brewer who'd opened a couple of spots in Colorado. Hennessey had a seven-barrel system, partially converted from a "Grundy" tank built in the United Kingdom. DeLange was surprised to get the call back from Ska. "It was the first time I experienced how helpful craft brewers in Colorado could be. I couldn't

Dry Dock's first bar reminded some people of an ice cream parlor. *Kevin DeLange.*

believe he had been thinking about it and made the effort to get in touch a week later," DeLange says.

Over the next few months—and with help from Rock Bottom's Hanley—DeLange convinced Aurora's zoning department to make a zoning exception for his "manufacturing" facility, installed the brewing system and purchased the rest of the equipment he would need. All told, it cost him $125,000, more than twice what he'd planned to pay.

When he finally opened on October 13, 2005, DeLange had six high-back chairs set up around an oak plywood bar in the corner of the Brew Hut. "It was the nicest thing we owned, including the brewing equipment," he says. There were ten beers on tap, including HMS Bounty Old Ale, Breakwater Pale Ale, Nut Brown, Enterprise IPA and Vanilla Porter. It was so small and sort of hidden that it reminded him of a speakeasy. And there was no sign and no real way for people to find out about the brewery unless they were already Brew Hut customers. As a result, Dry Dock sold almost nothing for the first six months. In fact, the brewery, named for DeLange's love of nautical history, sold less beer in a week back then than it does in a couple of hours today.

DeLange wondered what he'd gotten himself into.

And then came the 2006 World Beer Cup in Seattle. The event, held every two years by the Brewers Association, was and still is one of the largest and most important beer competitions in the world. DeLange attended, but when it was time for the awards, he was out in the hotel ballroom listening because he didn't want to pay for a dinner ticket. Somehow, among all of the famed breweries on hand, Dry Dock won a gold medal for DeLange's HMS Victory ESB in the special bitter or best bitter category. Rock Bottom's Hanley (who died in 2006) couldn't believe it. "Fucking homebrewers," he said to DeLange with a laugh and shake of his head.

At the time, there were fewer than one hundred microbreweries in Colorado and there just wasn't much going on in that world, so the fact that Dry Dock won gold was big news—big enough to appear above the fold in the print editions of both the *Rocky Mountain News* and the *Denver Business Journal*. "That award was the single most important moment in our history," Delange says. "It was the one thing that made us successful."

Now people were finding Dry Dock, and although DeLange had wanted to move to Arvada a few years earlier, he was happy he stayed in Aurora. "The roads leading to all the homes in the neighborhood funnel right into the intersection out front," he explains. "Aurora didn't have a brewery yet, but now we had a huge captive audience and the demographic was perfect. We just popped right into their backyard. The timing and the location were perfect."

By 2009, DeLange and Reding had upgraded their brewing equipment, expanded the taproom significantly and won another couple of medals (DeLange and Reding have since divorced, but they are still business partners, amicably running the brewery). They also hired "a real brewer" named Bill Eye. Although DeLange was good at recipe formulation, he didn't have the patience for the continuous struggle for consistency. Eye, on the other hand, loved to dial recipes in and perfect them. (Eye is now the co-owner of Bierstadt Lagerhaus, a highly respected German-style brewery in Denver).

Then, at GABF in 2009, Dry Dock took home three more medals and the Small Brewing Company and Small Brewing Company Brewer of the Year award.

In 2011, Dry Dock expanded again, turning that once tiny taproom into a beautifully decorated space with room for 170 people and barrel-aging program. DeLange also started self-distributing several of his beers to local liquor stores in twenty-two-ounce bomber bottles.

In 2013, the company bought a thirty-thousand-square-foot vacant warehouse in another section of Aurora and installed a new forty-barrel brewing system and a state-of-the-art canning line. Had it waited another year, that facility may have not been available thanks to the overwhelming demand for warehouses that the marijuana industry created that year. Dry Dock opened a second taproom there in 2014, and by the end of 2017, the brewery was pumping out nearly twenty-two thousand barrels per year, about 60 percent of that going into cans. By mid-2018, Dry Dock had filled about 19 million cans.

And Dry Dock has continued to win awards—seven at the World Beer Cup and twenty-four at GABF over ten straight years, more than any other Colorado brewery in that time period. These awards have come in for everything from the flagship Apricot Blonde to English ales like the S.S. Minnow Mild and the Enterprise English-style IPA, to German lagers, like pilsners, helle and marzens.

But Dry Dock hadn't just built something for itself. Without knowing it, DeLange and Reding ushered in a new wave of taprooms in Colorado that would change the way people drink beer in Colorado, change the culture of craft beer and kickstart an industry that has a $3 billion annual impact in the state. In 2008, Upslope Brewing opened a little taproom in Boulder. They were followed by several other taprooms, including Strange Craft in Denver, Funkwerks in Fort Collins and Crazy Mountain Brewing in the mountain town of Edwards, all in 2010.

In 2015, there were 352 active federal brewing licenses in Colorado, up from 104 the year Dry Dock opened. (The number of breweries was fewer than this because companies can own several licenses.) By 2017, there were 448, with a new brewery opening about once a week on average in the state. The vast majority were taprooms with no food.

Although Dry Dock is now one of the largest packaging breweries in the state, it began with almost nothing and showed people that they could open a brewery with not much money and without much experience. There are so many brewery taprooms now that the sheer number has begun to have a competitive effect on craft beer bars, dive bars and larger breweries. Many people skip the liquor stores these days and head straight or their local brewery where they can get a crowler, a six-pack or a few bottles to go.

And they are likely to be the future as well, says Steve Kurowski, formerly of the Colorado Brewers Guild, which represents about two-thirds of the state's breweries, especially as competition increases. "Tasting rooms will be the main profit center in Colorado," he says. "While a lower percentage will be packaging beer. The neighborhoods have supported this, and they continue to do so. So, hyper-local will be even more in play."

And surprise, surprise. Dry Dock may have scored with another strategy. While many regionally sized breweries—those that make more than fifteen thousand barrels per year—expanded distribution into other states during the mid-2010s, Dry Dock bucked the trend, focusing on Colorado. Now, as those bigger breweries struggle to find space on the shelf locally and to keep up sales in other states, which now boast their own regional breweries, Dry Dock has a strong position inside the state where it spends all of its resources.

"Ten years ago, Colorado beer was needed in the rest of the country," Kurowski points out. "But not anymore," not with more than eight thousand breweries in the United States. "Colorado's footprint is smaller. I'm sorry to see that change, but Denver is still a world-class beer city. With seventy-plus breweries, you're going to find something great no matter what."

16

STRANGE CRAFT AND TAPROOM REVOLUTION

It was a Monday afternoon in 2006, and Tim Myers needed to pick up some yeast for his latest batch of homebrew, but his regular shop, Beer at Home, wasn't open on Mondays. So, Myers headed across town—from Englewood to Aurora—to the next-closest store, the Brew Hut, which Kevin DeLange and Michelle Reding had purchased four years earlier.

Myers had been to the little shop before, but he noticed something different this time: a high counter in the back with some high-back chairs and a small menu board. "What's up with the ice cream parlor?" he asked, because that's what the setup looked like to him. The answer took him by surprise. It was a taproom where DeLange was selling beer by the pint.

"That was the first clue I had that something smaller than Great Divide or New Belgium could even be possible," Myers says. "That someone could have a taproom by itself."

Five years later, on May 19, 2010, Myers and former coworker John Fletcher opened Strange Brewing, later renamed Strange Craft Beer Company, under an overpass and next to the train tracks in an industrial area near Mile High Stadium, the home of the Denver Broncos. It was just the third new brewery in Denver in a decade and one of only nine or ten operating within the city limits at the time. And just as Dry Dock Brewing had done in Aurora, it became the first brewery in Denver to open as a taproom only—without either food or a packaging facility.

At the time, most people still thought beermakers needed one or the other to survive and to stay within the letter of the law. It turns out they didn't, and Myers and the half dozen or so breweries that followed his lead, including Wit's End Brewing, Caution Brewing, Renegade Brewing, Copper Kettle Brewing and Denver Beer Company, ushered in a new era of taproom-only breweries in the city that would see the number of beermakers grow from nine to more than seventy-five (depending on how you count) just eight years later.

While this new taproom model was slowly making its way across the country, it was still virtually unheard of in Colorado, aside from Dry Dock and one or two others. It was so novel in fact that when Julia Herz, the craft program director for the Brewers Association, heard about it, she asked Myers if he could time the opening with American Craft Beer Week in May so that the organization could properly applaud the new company.

Today, Strange is considered to be the grandfather of what former Colorado Brewers Guild director John Carlson calls the fourth wave of craft breweries in Denver (Carlson served the Guild for nearly twenty years). But it wasn't easy—in fact it was anything but. Myers likes to joke that Strange has been the poster child for "what not to do." Over the years, Myers has fought through zoning, permitting and licensing hurdles; a high-profile trademark battle; a name change; an ownership change; and equipment mistakes. Still,

Left to right: Scott Witsoe and Tyler Bies of Wit's End Brewing with Strange Craft's Tim Myers. *Emily Hutto.*

Strange has grown by 25 to 35 percent each year, won medals and accolades and built a reputation as an anchor in Denver's exploding taproom scene.

Myers's personality also helped set the tone for the collaborative, cooperative spirit that makes craft brewing so different from most other industries, says Jeremy Gobien, who opened Copper Kettle Brewing in Denver in May 2011 with his wife, Kristen Kozik. "Tim inspired a whole new wave of breweries that came after him that the dream was possible."

Rather than keeping his secrets to himself, Myers, who is rarely glimpsed without a smile and his signature Australian Outback hat, has helped or advised dozens of other breweries, lending or giving them his know-how and his encouragement or ingredients and equipment, sharing tips and strategies and welcoming competitors with open arms.

As Gobien tells it, he and Kozik had moved to Denver in the fall of 2009, just a month after getting married, and while he was finishing his PhD in engineering in North Carolina. But almost immediately, he realized that his real passion was brewing beer. So, Gobien began applying for entry-level work. "I would have been happy cleaning floors and helping with packaging if anyone would have given me a job," he remembers. "I think the people screening the resumes thought I was crazy taking a PhD education and applying for minimum wage jobs, but I was looking for someone to give me a chance to prove myself."

By May 2010, Gobien was pretty down on his prospects, so he and Kristen started to study the feasibility of opening their own brewery. Neither had any industry experience or any background in running a business, and the process was overwhelming.

"That's when we walked into the recently opened Strange Brewing" and struck up a conversation with Myers, Gobien says. "When we brought up the idea of opening a brewery of our own Tim wasn't just helpful, he was excited. He offered to sit down and explain his solutions to any problem we had, offered advice on how to make the process easier or better, and generally kept us encouraged and upbeat that we could succeed."

That infectious optimism and commonsense practicality made Myers popular with other would-be brewers who came to him for advice over the years. How much they appreciated his help was clear in 2012 when more than a dozen breweries rallied around Strange, holding a festival designed to raise money for legal fees. At the time, Strange was battling over its name with a Massachusetts homebrew shop with a similar moniker. The brewery eventually changed its name to Strange Craft, but the trademark fight helped bring Denver's brewing scene together.

The lessons that Myers was able to pass on came at a big cost, though.

Eleven years earlier, in 1999, Myers, an IT expert, was hired by the *Rocky Mountain News*—which was founded in April 23, 1859, just sixth months before the first brewery in town—to make sure that the storied old newspaper was ready for Y2K. Many technology experts at the time believed that computer systems across the world were going to melt down on January 1, 2000, when their digital clocks rolled over to 00. Myers, a contractor, was hired full-time at the *Rocky* afterward, and he met Fletcher, who also worked in IT.

The next year, when the *Rocky* merged with its longtime rival, the *Denver Post*, the two men stayed on. A few years later, the two papers decided to move into a new building on the edge of Denver's Civic Center Park. Myers and Fletcher were working 70 to 120 hours per week getting the new building ready. But in 2009, as newspaper subscriptions continued to decline in the face of the growing internet use, the *Rocky* shut down. It published its last edition on February 27, 2009, and laid off all of its employees.

"We were out of jobs and we had no credit, and we were in the middle of a recession," Myers says with a smile. "It was the perfect time to open a brewery."

Myers and Fletcher (who is no longer part of the brewery) had seen the writing on the wall. In fact, they'd been working on a business plan for a brewery for a while.

Back in 2005, while shopping online for Christmas presents for his stepdad, Myers had come across a Craigslist ad for a twenty-gallon brewing system with all the bells and whistles. "This guy in Boulder had bought it, but never really used it and it was sitting in his backyard filling up with pine needles. Myers bought the system, which had been around $8,000 new, for $2,000, along with a pair of fermentation tanks and about thirty or forty homebrewing books. He and some friends had started a homebrewing club a few years earlier and started using the new system. They would mash in thirty gallons, and then each member would take home five gallons and make a different recipe with the same wort. Myers developed some of the recipes he still uses and worked on being able to make exactly the same beer each time.

The goal of opening a brewery seemed a long way off, though, especially after Myers talked to existing brewery owners like Brian Dunn, the founder of Great Divide. Dunn's model from the beginning had been to package beers and sell growlers, and he suggested that Myers would need $2.5 to $3 million to get started. Myers had nothing close to that, which is why things changed so dramatically for him after he discovered Dry Dock's taproom.

Strange opened with that same twenty-gallon homebrew system, which meant Myers was making beer almost every single day for a year to keep up with the demand in the taproom. Some of his earliest staff were volunteers, and Myers and Fletcher didn't begin paying themselves for many months. Eventually, he upgraded his system—and upgraded it again—but it took a lot of time and energy and mistakes.

But it also showed other dreamers that a standalone brewery taproom was possible.

"Tim was a priceless resource we could turn to at any time," Jeremy Gobien says. "One of the most important concepts Tim showed us was the idea of opening a brewery with budgets regular people could afford—allowing us to open without the need for investors for funding."

In addition, he "enabled the explosion of Colorado breweries starting with a low cost, low overhead, low risk concept to grow into something larger, more labor efficient equipment as they matured and were able to reinvest in their businesses," he says. "Our choice for opening-day equipment was at a scale in between what Strange and Dry Dock used, however the cost was less than what many people would spend on a new car."

17

RIVER NORTH

Before it was Black Shirt Brewing, the brick building at the corner of Downing and Walnut Streets had been many things: a diesel engine repair shop, a disco in the '70s, a furniture warehouse, possibly even a brothel. But when brothers Chad and Branden Miller found it in late 2010, it was a vacant eyesore a block from the train tracks and surrounded by a hidden rhythm that most of Denver didn't hear and didn't see.

"We rode our bikes around to get a feel for the area," Branden says. "It was rough on the surface, but I never once felt endangered. It felt comfortable. There was a pulse to it that we understood."

The Millers and Chad's wife, Carissa, signed a lease for the four-thousand-square-foot building that year and took possession of it on New Year's Day in 2011. For the next twenty months, they gutted it and fixed it up, mostly by themselves, after working their other full-time jobs. They also met the locals and delved into both the past and present of what was being called the River North Art District.

"The first people we knew were the artist types, the musicians and sculptors and woodworkers. This was the cheapest space in Denver, so the art co-ops were here. Some of them were even squatting in empty buildings," Branden says. "It was wild and fun, and no one cared what was happening. We wanted to be part of it."

They had no idea how much it would change—and how quickly. Or how many other would-be brewers would be attracted to that same vibe. Today, the River North Arts District, or RiNo, is one of the trendiest areas of Denver,

Black Shirt Brewing was founded in River North Arts District in 2012. *Black Shirt Brewing.*

filled with condominium complexes (both finished and under construction), offices, workspaces, cocktail bars, clubs, restaurants and parking problems. It has also been home to more than a dozen breweries (as well as cideries and wineries) since 2011, with more on the way.

Born and raised in the southwestern Colorado town of Westcliffe, the Miller brothers grew up in a working-class Colorado family, and they took an interest in winemaking and beer brewing early on. Chad moved to Denver in 2000 to work first in the collision repair and later in commercial real estate. Branden followed in 2002, taking front-of-house jobs in several restaurants. Quiet, serious-minded and passionate, the brothers both wear black and channel a Johnny Cash meets punk rock vibe. They spend a lot of time and energy and thought on everything they do—and they put that same effort into designing the brewery. The bar and tabletops, for instance, are made from the reused flooring of boxcars that used to run on the nearby railroad tracks. The table legs are made from old shelving uprights that were used in a warehouse down the street. A small stage on the back patio is built entirely from wooden pallets.

Out front is a forty-five-foot marquis that came with the building. During renovation, the Millers decided to paint their brewery name on it, but as

Chad cleaned it up and chipped away at the old paint, he realized that there were words written underneath. "He'd spent all day out there, chipping away. He was like an archaeologist," Branden says. Eventually, the words "Johnson and Loud" revealed themselves like time travelers from the 1950s when the building was a thriving furniture showroom and warehouse. Black Shirt painted its initials on the marquis, but kept the ghost sign, which is still clearly visible.

It was a small piece of a fascinating history, but the story of the neighborhood, just a few blocks from the South Platte River, goes back a lot further than that—back to Denver's founding in 1858.

Denver was born on a river, because of a river, and in spite of a river. But the residents of the city never gave much back to their watery parents, the South Platte and the Cherry Creek. The South Platte, in particular, has taken a lot of abuse. In the 1880s, the rail lines finally arrived, running along both sides of the river. Rail-reliant industries followed, including the stockyards, which are still there today, ore smelters, foundries, meat packing plants, brickyards and warehouses. For them, the river was simply an easy dumping ground.

To support these operations, a host of working-class towns and neighborhoods sprang up adjacent to the heavy industry to house employees, who would walk to work. On the west side of the river was Globeville, populated mainly by eastern European and Russian immigrants. On the east side were Elyria and Swansea and, just to south, the Cole neighborhood. These areas were populated with immigrants from Germany, Poland, Italy, Ireland and Slavic nations. Although the work was hard, these communities were dynamic near the turn of the twentieth century, packed full of churches, markets, schools, hotels, banks, dance halls and street cars. And there were plenty of saloons serving lager beer from the likes of Tivoli and Zang's.

After World War II, the neighborhoods changed. Returning GIs discovered that the increasingly industrialized world had moved on, and they couldn't hold the same jobs as their parents and grandparents. So, the families that had settled Globeville, Swansea, Elyria and Cole moved on as well—to Denver's suburbs. They were quickly replaced by Latino immigrants, happy to find decent housing in the city.

The industries along the South Platte changed too. Manufacturers and machine shops moved in, along with chemical companies, painters, auto mechanics, transportation hubs, tow yards and junkyards to handle the remains of the burgeoning automobile industry.

And still, they used the South Platte as a dumping ground.

By the early 1960s, locals had forgotten a lesson their predecessors learned a century earlier when a series of floods destroyed the early settlements that would later become Denver: the river can sometimes fight back. In May and June 1965, a series of intense storms like no one had seen pounded the foothills to the west and the plains to the north and east. As the rain continued to fall, creeks and tributaries began to swell, most jumping their banks. Then, on June 16, a wall of water built up in the South Platte south of Denver. It rose higher and higher until it swept through the core of city. The worst natural disaster in Denver's history, the flood killed twenty-one people, caused billions of dollars (in today's money) in damage, knocked down thirteen urban viaducts and bridges, destroyed hundreds of homes and businesses and swamped 250,000 acres of land.

One of the casualties was Tivoli Brewing, where nine feet of water flooded the basement, causing $135,000 in damages (or roughly half a million in today's money). If the Neef Brothers and Zang breweries, had still been standing in their original spots near the river, the water would have flooded them as well. Tivoli would recover, but not enough. The brewery closed in 1969.

Globeville was also hit hard, but the rest of north Denver was spared the brunt of the damage. Still, the flood of '65 would change the way the city saw its river and the course of city's future.

As a result of the flood, three major dams were built. In 1974, then-mayor Bill McNichols formed a committee to revitalize the Platte River corridor. Over the next twenty-five years, the Greenway Foundation helped steer $500 million in new investment into parks, trails and projects that would renew the waterway. A walking and biking path now lines the river, along with gardens, murals and condominium complexes.

But even by 2000, the river was still in bad shape, as it wound through the now very low-income neighborhoods of Globeville, Elyria and Swansea and out of town. To make matters worse, government officials decided to run Interstate 70 through the middle of Elyria, Swansea and Globeville in 1964, dividing these neighborhoods in half and separating them from the rest of Denver.

Polluted and ignored, the industrial areas bordering the river had little infrastructure and were still populated by vacant lots, unwanted business and empty warehouses. Homeless people used the Platte as both a laundry bin and a latrine. Abandoned furniture and car parts littered the banks.

But one person's trashy urban wasteland is another's inspiration. In 1999, four artists bought an old garage at Thirty-Sixth and Chestnut and rehabbed it into a sculpture, painting and woodworking studio space and gallery called Ironton. They named it for a long-gone 1890s-era school that had been nearby and had served the German, Swedish, Scottish, Irish and Slavic children of Denver smelter employees. In 2000, artist Tracy Weil built a unique home across the street from Ironton on the banks of the river. Other artists followed, attracted to the cheap rent, the gritty nature of the neighborhood and its proximity to downtown.

In 2005, Weil and artist Jill Hadley-Hooper, who had joined Ironton, took inspiration from other art districts in the city and wondered if they could start one here. So, they drew a large and awkward-looking circle around the studios and galleries owned by their friends and formed the River North Arts District, taking the name from a recently implemented rebuilding plan that city officials had begun talking about. To add some flair, the artists called it RiNo and used a whimsical rhinoceros as a logo.

That circle would change the face of the city forever.

The district stretches along Interstate 70 to the north, with Interstate 25 and Park Avenue as its western borders down to the edge of Coors Field. Then it heads northeast along the alley between Larimer and Lawrence Streets before cutting a slightly more jagged path back up to I-70. The circle overlaps large chunks of Globeville, Elyria, Swansea and Five Points, as well as a small part of Cole. It also includes parts of business-centric areas, such as the Upper Larimer District and the Ballpark neighborhood. The river and the railroad and some new light rail tracks bisect it from top to bottom, creating several odd and difficult-to-reach islands that don't connect well to the other areas.

Although River North's founders continue to stress that their boundaries make up an art district rather than a neighborhood—and they try to respect the historic neighborhoods as much as they can—the area is most often referred to as a neighborhood locally and nationally. Ironically, it has more housing now than it ever did before. "People got excited about it, and about the name," Weil says. "It's hard to control at this point."

Matt and Jessica Hess were definitely excited about it when they began combing the streets of River North in 2011, looking for a spot to open their brewery. "We loved it and we could see the potential there," Matt says. "We were looking for a nice visible spot with a cool feel to it." That spot turned out to be the corner of Twenty-Fourth and Blake Streets, just two blocks from Coors Field, on the very edge of RiNo. But with a marketing savvy that would turn out to be brilliant, they named their new business after the art district. River North Brewery opened in February 2012, serving Belgian-style ales from saisons and a wit to a Quadrupel and a stout.

Matt and Jessica Hess founded River North Brewery in 2012. *Sarah Cowell.*

The building Hess leased already had all the infrastructure needed for a brewery, but at the time, he had no idea why. It turns out that it had a noble Denver brewing history—it had been home to Timberline Brewing and Broadway Brewing in the 1990s. After that, Flying Dog Brewing took over in 2000, before moving to Maryland in 2008. At that point, Flying Dog owner George Stranahan decided to keep the building and turn it into a whisky distillery, founding Stranahan's Colorado Whiskey. But when Stranahan's moved in 2009, the building at 2401 Blake Street sat vacant until Hess found it and renovated it once again.

"We were lucky that our original location was small and we could focus on a niche that we were excited about and on the Belgian styles that I really loved brewing," says Hess, who was raised in Kansas and went to school in Missouri before joining the aerospace industry for nine years. "And we exceeded where we thought we would be in the first couple years, so that was exciting."

But in 2015, the building's brewing history came to an end. Its owner sold the property to a luxury condo developer who evicted River North Brewery

Before it was demolished, River North Brewery's first home also held Broadway Brewing and Flying Dog Brewing. *Matt Hess.*

and tore the structure down. To honor the original building, River North Brewery salvaged a brick from demolition day and gave it to the Falling Rock Taphouse, which displayed it on a wall. Hess had to scramble to move his business to a new spot in north Denver for several years, but by the end of 2018, he was building a new taproom back in old neighborhood, at 3400 Blake Street, just ten blocks from the original and just three blocks from Black Shirt. It opened in early 2019.

"We had no idea how quickly the neighborhood would take off. And the number of breweries that opened there in just a few years was amazing," Hess says. "We were fortunate to be a part of it."

Though River North Brewery and Black Shirt were the first two beermakers to open in the district, they would be far from the last. Our Mutual Friend Brewing, like Black Shirt, opened during the Great American Beer Festival week in 2012. A year later, Utah-based Epic Brewing opened a large taproom and production facility and was followed by Crooked Stave Artisan Beer Project, Mockery Brewing, Beryl's Beer Company, Zephyr Brewing, Ratio Beerworks, Bierstadt Lagerhaus, 14er Brewing and a Denver outpost of Fort Collins–based Odell Brewing. New Belgium Brewing, meanwhile, opened a pilot brewhouse and wood-barrel aging facility on the eighth floor of the Source Hotel in late 2018. And Great Divide Brewing, running out of room in its twenty-year-old brewery near Coors Field purchased land on the banks of the river where it opened a new tasting room and packaging facility in 2014.

So popular is River North, in fact, that it attracted the two largest beermakers in the United States. In 2016, Bend, Oregon's 10 Barrel Brewing, now owned by Anheuser-Busch InBev, opened a brewpub at Twenty-Sixth and Walnut Streets, while Coors's storied Blue Moon Brewing opened a multimillion-dollar showplace pub and brewery of its own the same year at Thirty-Eighth Street and Walnut Place.

But all that competition took a toll. In 2017, Zephyr Brewing moved out of RiNo to a production facility north of the city and later closed. In 2018, Beryl's closed up shop and was replaced by 14er Brewing. Crooked Stave will also leave RiNo in 2020, returning to its former home in Denver's Sunnyside neighborhood.

Still, the district has become the number-one destination in the city for beer tourists and locals looking for the latest style innovations and trends. It is also known as a place where beer lovers can walk or bike to multiple spots in a single afternoon or evening. A light rail station opened in 2017, and a pedestrian bridge now crosses the old railroad tracks to connect RiNo's two sides.

18

SOUR BEER AND SOCIAL MEDIA

May 26, 2012, was clear and hot in Denver. The day before, the temperature had reached seventy-five degrees Fahrenheit, but by 11:00 a.m. on this Saturday, the needle on the thermometer was already nudging past eighty degrees on the way up to ninety-two, an unseasonable springtime scorcher. Outside the Falling Rock Taphouse, a couple dozen excited beer drinkers, mostly men, had gathered to wait in a line. There were a lot of beards, a lot of cargo shorts and a lot of T-shirts that didn't quite fit.

It was bottle-release day for the Cellar Reserve membership of Crooked Stave Artisan Beer Project, a brewery that was even hotter than that day's sunshine. Founded in 2010 by yeast expert Chad Yakobson, Crooked Stave didn't even have a taproom yet—it was brewing its beer at Funkwerks, a saison specialist in Fort Collins, but that didn't matter. Yakobson was making a distinct kind of beer that almost no other U.S. brewer had tried: sour ales.

Brewed in Europe for several hundred years, sour and "wild" ales are part of several regional brewing traditions but are most often associated with Belgium and, to a lesser degree, Germany. They are usually fermented by Brettanomyces yeast, which occurs naturally, though most breweries rely on carefully domesticated brewers' yeasts and avoid Brett because of the wide and often unexpected flavors it imparts into beer. These flavors are often described as funky, earthy or musty. The words "hay-like" and "horse barn" are even used.

Beers brewed with Brett are known now as wild ales. To make a beer truly sour, though, brewers add bacterial agents like *Pediococcus* and *Lactobacillus*, which raise the acidity level. Sours can range from mildly tart to mouth-puckeringly aggressive. To many people, the seemingly infinite variety of flavors and aromas resulting from the Brett and the bacteria are difficult to get used to or are just plain gross. To others, they are heaven.

In Colorado, only a handful of breweries, like New Belgium, Avery, Trinity and Odell had made serious efforts to brew sour or wild ales. Most were sporadic or seasonal. Nationwide, Jolly Pumpkin, Allagash, Russian River and a few others had experimented with sours, but the majority came from Belgian breweries like Cantillon, Tilquin, Oud Beersel and 3 Fonteinen.

Yakobson's plans went far beyond what was being done in the United States. His goal was to make only 100 percent Brettanomyces beers—all fermented in wooden barrels. Most would also be sours, and the majority would be brewed with added fruit.

Raised in the Colorado foothills, Yakobson studied winemaking at Colorado State University before moving to New Zealand, where he planned to get his master's degree in viticulture. Instead, he fell in love with beer, particularly sour beer, and enrolled at Heriot-Watt University in Scotland, where he wrote his master's thesis on the characteristics of Brettanomyces yeast and its use in brewing.

Basically, he got a degree in beer.

Crooked Stave's Chad Yakobson. *Dustin Hall/The Brewtography Project.*

Afterward, Yakobson moved to Fort Collins, got a job at Odell Brewing and struck up a friendship with Peter Bouckaert, the renowned New Belgium brewmaster. Bouckaert had moved from Belgium to Fort Collins in 1996 and pioneered sour beer–making in America when he introduced La Folie, a Flanders-style brown.

"I knew so much about Brett," Yakobson says. "But Peter said, it's great that you've done all of this research, but what does it mean?" Bouckaert wanted to know if an American brewer could ever make sour beers on a regular basis. Was it something a brewer could produce as a flagship beer and sell to people as an everyday drink?

"That question is the core of what started Crooked Stave," Yakobson says.

The answer was a resounding yes. Over the next few years, Crooked Stave helped create the market for this style, not just in Colorado but also nationwide. Yakobson forged new pathways in the use of Brett and fruit and wooden barrels. He traveled the world, lecturing on yeast and collaborating on beers with brewers in several countries.

Today, there are half a dozen or so breweries in Colorado that only make wild and sour ales, including Black Project Wild & Spontaneous Ales, Casey Brewing and Blending, Paradox Beer Company, Cellar West Artisan Ales and Primitive. But dozens of others, both large and small, have tried their hand at it, some developing large and respected sour programs. They include old hands like Avery, Odell and Great Divide, along with newer breweries like Epic, TRVE Brewing, Baere Brewing, Our Mutual Friend, Wiley Roots, Odd13 Brewing and Funkwerks.

Along with the beer, Yakobson also helped create a new kind of beer drinker—dedicated, sometimes rabid, social media–enabled uber-fans. Pejoratively referred to as fanboys and fangirls, they are educated, opinionated and mercurial, and they don't mind standing in long lines to get their favorite liquids, usually shelling out hundreds of dollars for just a few bottles (or cans). Many also trade beer or buy and sell on the aftermarket—something that is technically illegal but widespread, nonetheless.

For Crooked Stave, which had garnered attention despite having barely produced anything yet, the madness began in late 2011 when Yakobson announced that the brewery would start a membership club called Cellar Reserve. For $300 a year, fans who signed up were guaranteed a certain amount of rare sour beers, as well as glassware, T-shirts, a tin tacker and tote bags—and the rights to buy more beer.

Only a few other breweries across the country, including the Bruery and Lost Abbey, both in California, had done something similar at the time (though these clubs are now everywhere). The clubs not only raised money, but they also created hype.

"We had 166 members that first year. We had hoped for more. But really it was the perfect amount," Yakobson says. "The enthusiasm was wonderful to see. People traveled from out of state to pick up beer. I was nothing short of amazing to see that kind of passion for a product that I was also so passionate about. It draws even more creativity out of you."

It was a unique time in the industry's history. The craft beer renaissance that would see 250 breweries open in Colorado between 2010 and 2018 was just taking shape, and taproom culture was in its infancy. Denver itself boasted about a dozen breweries—with ten more in planning—but no one imagined how many more were on their way and how quickly they would arrive.

"Looking back, Denver was really young in its craft beer evolution, and I think we helped shape it as each new brewery opened," Yakobson says. "As for sours, Denver was a great jumping off point for that. Crooked Stave made Colorado a hotbed for the style."

On that hot May day outside the Falling Rock in 2012, Yakobson and his team, mostly volunteers and family members, sat under portable sunshades and handed bottles to Cellar Reserve members, who had to hustle home to keep them cold. The beers that Crooked Stave released were Petite Sour, a blend of oak-aged beers aged with Brett and *Lactobacillus*, and Persica, a sour golden ale aged in oak barrels with peaches and Brett.

A few months later, Yakobson opened a small taproom and barrel-aging facility (he actually brewed his beer at other breweries nearby) where people would line up for each new release. In May 2013, Crooked Stave hosted Roy G. Biv Day (an acronym for a series of seven Brett beers) with a bottle sale, a party and a couple of rare beer tappings. "There were four to five hundred people in line wrapped around the building," Yakobson recalls. "We ran out of beer with forty or fifty people to go still. We sold more than one hundred cases that day."

Crooked Stave's creations were delicious—the product of years of research and dedication—but Yakobson knows that some of their popularity also had to do with being in the right place at the right time. Not only were sours rare and highly sought after, but beer fans were also increasingly interested in seeking out hard-to-find beers of any style and then bragging about them online. Many of these whales, or "walez," as they are often called on social media, in a play on the hunt for Moby Dick, attracted a cult following and were discussed at length, hyped, traded and bought and sold, often at a profit. (Crooked Stave even produced a beer called Waelzblood in 2013 for returning members of the Cellar Reserve.)

Other states had similar breweries, like California's Russian River, where people lined up by the hundreds for Pliny the Younger, and Lost Abbey, where they jostled one another for a bottle of Angel's Share, as well as Indiana's 3 Floyds, where they stayed out all night for Dark Lord. And although Colorado already had great breweries too, "there was never really one that they latched onto like us, that they could buy from and be able to trade for other beers," Yakobson says. "We were making beers that really weren't available anywhere else, and people were proud. Crooked Stave was new and exciting, and a community was born. We embraced that culture."

Before Crooked Stave, lines had been rare in Colorado. Avery Brewing in Boulder certainly commanded attention and long lines for its barrel-aged sours and special releases. Bristol Brewing in Colorado Springs had people queuing every fall for its Venetucci Pumpkin Ale. And in 2012, more than one hundred people lined up for the chance to join the Growler Cvlt at TRVE Brewing, which hadn't even officially opened yet. A few of the geekiest beer geeks also stood in line for small-batch beers, typically bourbon barrel–aged stouts from other beermakers like River North Brewery, Station 26 Brewing and Oskar Blues.

True line culture didn't really begin until a couple of years later, though. In 2014, Troy Casey, who, like his father, had worked for MillerCoors, opened Casey Brewing and Blending in the mountain town of Glenwood Springs, where he specialized in sour and wild ales. Like Yakobson, Casey brewed elsewhere and brought the unfermented wort back to his brewery where he inoculated it with Brett and bacteria and aged and blended it with fruit.

Soon after opening, hundreds of people from Denver and Boulder began making the three-and-a-half-hour drive for his once-a-month releases.

That same year, Black Project Wild & Spontaneous Ales in Denver (then called Former Future Brewing) began turning out award-winning sours that attracted a lot of people. Lines for their releases began forming in the wee hours of the night—even during winter when sleeping bags were a must—along a sometimes-sketchy stretch of South Broadway.

Like Yakobson, Black Project cofounder James Howat attended Colorado State University in Fort Collins and fell in love with sours by drinking New Belgium La Folie.

"I always liked things that are more on the acidic side. I would go for Skittles over M&Ms every time. That's just how my palate is," Howat explains.

People would camp out for hours to get Black Project's beers. *Jonathan Shikes.*

He and his then-wife and business partner, Sarah, opened Former Future Brewing in 2014, making a wide variety of non-sour beers, but their goal was always to make sours—and not just any kind of sours. Howat, a microbiology major, was fascinated by the idea of spontaneous fermentation, which is something the Belgians have been doing for hundreds of years. To spontaneously ferment a beer, the brewer brews a batch of wort and then leaves it overnight with exposure to the air during the colder months. Naturally occurring yeast and bacteria inoculate the beer and begin the fermentation process, adding wild, funky, fruity, dry and sour flavors and aromas.

"You can have a beer with hundreds of different species in it—which is so drastically different from making pitched beers," Howat explains.

From the beginning, Howat experimented with spontaneous fermentation, lugging two giant cauldrons to the roof of his brewery and pumping hot wort into them from below. Then he'd let them gather whatever microorganisms Denver's night air had to offer. Former Future released the first of these in late 2014 using a separate name, Black Project, to differentiate the beer from Former Futures' offerings. It immediately won a medal at GABF. Then he

James Howat of Black Project Wild & Spontaneous Ales. *Jonathan Shikes.*

released a second and a third and won another medal. By 2015, people were lining up on release days to buy whatever tiny amounts of spontaneously fermented beer Howat could make. So, after a lot of thought, James and Sarah took a huge risk—they ditched the Former Future name in favor of Black Project Wild & Spontaneous Ales and switched their focus entirely to spontaneously fermented sours.

Their customer base immediately turned over. About 90 percent of their taproom regulars didn't really like sour beers, although a few stuck around. Black Project developed a whole new base, some of whom visited Denver just to try the beers.

"We got lots of people who flew in from wherever and said, 'This is the one bar I had to visit,'" Howat recalls. "We had people who come straight from the airport with their rolling suitcases."

Some of those visitors were turning around and selling or trading that beer on the aftermarket for highly elevated prices, something that gives Howat mixed feelings.

"I'm somewhat laissez faire. Ideologically, I feel like people should be able to do it, but it's illegal, and it can make a brewery feel used," he says. "A small group of people determine the secondary value for those beers, and a lot of guys treat it like the stock market." What Howat really wants is for people to open the bottles and enjoy the beer.

In 2016, two other beer styles that had been creating a stir nationwide made their way to Colorado in force and sparked a full-blown explosion in line culture, social media hype and aftermarket sales. The first was New England–style IPAs, which are hazy, more tropical and much less bitter than traditional IPAs. The second was imperial or barrel-aged stouts made with adjuncts like vanilla beans, cacao, coconut or other sweet or dessert-like flavorings.

As they had done with Casey Brewing, Denver beer geeks drove in hordes to Odd13 Brewing in Lafayette, which specializes in New England–style IPAs, and Weldwerks Brewing in Greeley, which specializes in both of these new beers. In Denver, Cerebral Brewing also garnered enormous lines for its New England–style IPAs and stouts. Similar things were happening around the country, from Brooklyn to Los Angeles, from North Carolina to Massachusetts.

Victorious beer hunters would post pictures on social media to brag about the vast quantities of beer, especially New England–style IPAs, they'd scored that day. Garrett Oliver, the well-respected author and brewmaster at Brooklyn Brewery, called New England–style IPAs "the first beer based around Instagram culture."

Black Project, Casey, Cerebral, Weldwerks and other breweries eventually turned to lottery or ticket systems to cut down on the lines and the line culture that had been created by their releases. People were cutting in line, engaging in intimidation or hiring stand-ins to wait for them. The frenzy created a lot of bad will and it didn't exactly thrill neighboring businesses.

But the rush for rare and delicious beers can be a double-edge sword. For Yakobson, the internet hype has mostly moved on. In 2012 and 2013, he was a celebrity and his beers were selling out before they could even hit store shelves. Since then, competition has increased significantly, though, and times have changed. "Bottles go into stores and sit there like shelf art," he says. "None of us can control consumer trends or hype."

Crooked Stave has changed too. Yakobson has turned over day-to-day operations to his wife, Yetta, while the brewery itself has increased its production significantly since the early days and opened a second taproom, this one in Fort Collins, in 2019. It also started producing non-sour and non-wild ales, including a traditional keller pilsner, a Baltic porter infused with coffee and several New England–style IPAs.

19

THE MEANING OF INDEPENDENCE

In November 2014, when Anheuser-Busch InBev announced that it was purchasing Oregon craft darling 10 Barrel Brewing, the news came as a surprise, but it didn't scare anyone. Industry observers had speculated for a long time about when and how the big breweries would decide to get into the craft game. So far, AB InBev, which had grown from its German immigrant roots in the 1850s in St. Louis into a multibillion-dollar conglomerate based in Belgium, had purchased Chicago's Goose Island Brewing and New York's Blue Point Brewing, but until 2014, it hadn't made other craft overtures.

When Elysian Brewing, a craft pioneer that was founded in Seattle in 1995, sold out to AB InBev just three months later, though, it sent shockwaves through the industry. Two rapid purchases in the heart of the Pacific Northwest's beer country. Suddenly, it seemed like craft brewers might have awakened a giant—one with almost unlimited financial means.

Consolidation in the beer business certainly wasn't new. It had happened in the 1890s when English investment groups bought up dozens of U.S. breweries and again in the 1950s through the 1980s as the big breweries gobbled up hundreds of smaller breweries and brands. But this was different because craft breweries were founded in part as a rejection of consolidation.

The Brewers Association had been battling with "big beer" for years at that point, fighting in both the nation's capital and in individual state legislatures anytime a large beer company or distributor tried to pass a law that might hurt craft breweries. While Bud, Miller and Coors and their subsidiaries were welcome to enter their beers—and pay for expensive sponsorships—at the Great American Beer Festival, they weren't welcome in the BA. In fact, a few years earlier, the organization had defined a "craft" brewer, and thus a voting member, as "small and independent"; having an annual production of less than six million barrels; and, most controversially, as having no more than 25 percent ownership "by an alcoholic beverage industry member who is not themselves a craft brewer." That meant no Goose Island, Blue Point, Blue Moon or the Sandlot, 10 Barrel or Elysian.

A few years earlier, in 2012, the organization, representing 70 percent of the nation's craft brewers, had also upped its rhetoric when it came to big beer brands that didn't identify their ownership on their labels. In a treatise that became known as Craft vs. Crafty, the BA accused the large brewers of purposely creating "craft-imitating beers" as a way to gain entry into the niche. "Many non-standard, non-light 'crafty' beers found in the marketplace today are not labeled as products of large breweries. So, when someone is drinking a Blue Moon Belgian Wheat Beer, they often believe that it's from a craft brewer, since there is no clear indication that it's made by SABMiller. The same goes for Shock Top, a brand that is 100 percent owned by Anheuser-Busch InBev," the BA wrote. "The large, multinational brewers appear to be deliberately attempting to blur the lines between their crafty, craft-like beers and true craft beers from today's small and independent brewers. We call for transparency in brand ownership and for information to be clearly presented in a way that allows beer drinkers to make an informed choice about who brewed the beer they are drinking."

The BA plunged forward, telling consumers in 2014 that its goal was to help craft breweries attain 20 percent of the market share for beer in the United States by 2020. But as the calendar turned to 2015, that hope looked like it would be doomed. After buying Elysian, AB InBev went on to purchase California's Golden Road Brewing. MillerCoors, meanwhile, acquired San Diego's Saint Archer Brewing. That was followed by two dramatic sellouts. In September, the nation's sixth-largest craft brewery, Lagunitas, sold to Heineken. Then, in November, Constellation Brands, which makes Corona and Modelo, bought San Diego's Ballast Point, the nation's thirty-first-largest craft brewery. The sale price: $1 billion. (Constellation has since sold Ballast Point to an investment group.)

Since the BA had backed itself into a corner with its craft beer definition, it now had to strip voting rights from those members who it no longer considered craft. It also had to eliminate their sales and volume numbers from its annual tally of craft market share.

The Brewers Association rolled out its Independence Matters campaign in 2017. *Courtesy of the Brewers Association.*

By the end of 2015, people wondered who would be next. Would it be a Colorado brewery? Would New Belgium sell? What about Odell or Left Hand or Great Divide?

In December 2015, the question was answered.

Breckenridge Brewery was founded in 1990 by Richard Squire, an entrepreneur who had made some money in the clothing business back east and decided to ditch it all for the life of a Colorado ski bum and a homebrewer. Like many brewery owners who would come after him, friends kept telling him that his beer was good enough to be sold to the public. So, in 1990, Squire, who died in 2019, opened his brewpub on Main Street in the ski town of Breckenridge, where it is still located.

A businessman at heart, Squire opened a second spot the next year on a downtrodden stretch of Denver's Blake Street near Twenty-Second Street, just six blocks from Wynkoop Brewing. It was a good choice. In 1990, Denver was one of several cities vying for a new Major League Baseball expansion team, and local boosters had already picked a proposed downtown site—the blocks bounded by Twentieth and Twenty-Second Streets, Blake and Wewatta. Major League Baseball picked Denver in 1991, and the construction of Coors Field was completed in 1995.

Business, which had been hit or miss up to that point, boomed across the street at Breckenridge.

In 1994, Squire promoted one of his earliest employees, Todd Usry, to the spot of head brewer. He also hired a young go-getter named Todd Thibault on the sales side. The two Todds would help elevate Breckenridge to new heights.

The next year, the brewery gathered a new group of investors to finance the opening of a large production and bottling facility and a small barbecue restaurant at 471 Kalamath Street in Denver. At the same time, Squire began opening Breckenridge pubs in other states, including Buffalo, New York; Dallas, Texas; and Memphis, Tennessee. But within a couple of years, it was clear that the pubs weren't working, and the company closed or sold most of them. Squire himself, a mercurial visionary with little time for day-to-day details, began to cede power and ownership of the brewery to his investors, one of whom was lawyer Ed Cerkovnik, who became president of the company.

In the 2000s, Breckenridge expanded distribution across the country, building heavily on its Avalanche Ale brand and later on beers like Vanilla

Breckenridge Brewery built a huge new campus in 2015. *Jonathan Shikes.*

Porter, Agave Wheat and 471 IPA. It also opened several restaurants and brewpubs across the state. During that time, Breckenridge built on its long-standing reputation as a strong supporter and advocate for other small breweries as a staunchly independent craft brewer (Breckenridge even made a series of videos making fun of big beer brands like Coors, Miller, Bud and Corona) and as a charitable donor.

But by 2010, the brewery was at a crossroads. Although its beer was well known across the country, its brands had fallen behind the times and the company was facing serious competition from newer craft breweries. So, that year, Breckenridge, led by Cerkovnik, and Wynkoop Holdings, led by Lee Driscoll, who had taken control of the that brewery after John Hickenlooper became mayor of Denver, agreed to merge the two brewpub stalwarts. The combined entity, Breckenridge-Wynkoop Holdings, owned four brewpubs and nine restaurants.

It seemed like a good match: Breck's brewing capacity and bottling could feed Wynkoop's restaurants, providing a nice point to the other's counterpoint. But there were problems from the beginning. For starters, with the advent of craft brewing's popularity, demand for Breckenridge beers increased rapidly, and the company went from making about thirty-one thousand barrels of beer in 2010 to nearly twice that just two years later.

That would have been a good problem, except for a pair of pitfalls. The first was that Breckenridge's headquarters on Kalamath Street was running at capacity and was almost out of room. The second was a Colorado law that prohibited beer manufacturers with a brewpub license from producing more than 1,860,000 gallons—or 60,000 barrels—of beer per year. The cap had been put into place in 1996 as part of the new brewpub license classification. It was a way to placate distributors who relied on the three-tier system and didn't like the idea of brewpubs being able to sell beer directly to consumers without going through them.

To deal with the of lack of space, Cerkovnik, Driscoll and Usry began looking for a ten-acre spot in the metro area where they could build a proposed $15 million, 125,000-square-foot facility capable of brewing at least 100,000 barrels of beer per year.

For the second problem, they hired a lobbyist in 2012 to plead their case to the state legislature, asking lawmakers to increase the brewpub cap to 300,000 barrels. They assumed the change would be a lock. After all, Breckenridge was a homegrown success story and one of the oldest and largest craft breweries in an industry that generated $446 million for the state economy that year. And even though it was by far the biggest brewpub in the state, Breckenridge certainly didn't represent any kind of threat to distributors since it still sold all of its packaged beer through them.

But the opposition was fierce, not just from the wholesalers but also from restaurateurs and some of Breckenridge's own friends, like New Belgium Brewing and Odell Brewing, who believed the change would give Breckenridge an unfair advantage. While those two breweries didn't have to deal with the manufacturing cap, they weren't allowed to serve food like a brewpub.

These stances shocked and angered Usry, who was barely able to talk about it. "We are not out to take over the brewpub business in Colorado, by any stretch. You'd be hard-pressed to find a brewery in the state that has been nicer, or more about community, than us," he told *Westword* at the time. When the bill died, he and Cerkovnik threatened to move the company out of state.

Instead, Breckenridge-Wynkoop came to a complicated arrangement with the Colorado Department of Revenue, which handles liquor law enforcement. Since the company owned five brewpubs and each was allowed to make sixty thousand barrels of beer per year, Breckenridge created what's called an "alternating proprietorship" with the other breweries. Alternating proprietorships allow one brewery to loan or rent its equipment and its physical premises to another brewery for a certain period of time. They're designed to "allow existing breweries to use excess capacity and give new entrants to the beer business an opportunity to begin on a small scale, without investing in premises and equipment," according to the federal Alcohol Tobacco and Trade Bureau. But there was nothing to prevent two breweries owned by the same company from benefiting from the law as well—and that's just what Breckenridge-Wynkoop did.

As a result, Breckenridge would be able to brew up to sixty thousand barrels of beer for each of its three brewpubs, in addition to sixty thousand barrels of its own. It wasn't ideal, but the construct allowed Breckenridge to move forward on its expansion. In 2014, the company unveiled plans to build a twelve-acre, $36 million campus on the banks of the South Platte River in Littleton, just south of Denver. When it was completed in June 2015, the gorgeous, farm-like facility included a two-story, seventy-six thousand square-foot brewery and cellar, a one-hundred-barrel state-of-the-art Steinecker brewhouse, sixteen four-hundred-barrel fermenters and six silos (each capable of storing two semi-loads of grain). It also boasted new bottling and canning lines, a sixty-five-seat taproom, a six-hundred-person restaurant with a wrap-around patio with views of the mountains, a two-acre hop farm and a stage for music.

Just as they had done in the mid-1990s when the Wynkoop needed money to expand into other states, Lee Driscoll and his family helped create the financing for this project. But it wasn't easy, it wasn't cheap and it came just as the market for craft beer began to soften.

Which is why a few people weren't exactly shocked when Breckenridge-Wynkoop announced five months later that it would sell Breckenridge Brewery to AB InBev. But the rest were indeed shocked. For some employees and for thousands of loyal drinkers, there was a real sense of loss, even betrayal, that the fiercely independent company would sell to the very conglomerate that many people thought was trying to put craft brewers out of business. And they expressed themselves online, on social media, in letters to newspapers and directly to Usry and his crew.

The sale was difficult to swallow for many other breweries as well, especially those who stood arm in arm with Breckenridge over the years, battling big beer.

Todd Usry (*right*) was with Breckenridge Brewery from the beginning. *Anheuser-Busch InBev.*

"It's a sad day when someone like that, who has been fighting the fight for more than twenty years, sells out. For me, it is inconceivable," Left Hand Brewing cofounder Eric Wallace told *Westword* at the time. "How do you sell out to those guys? They are the ones who caused the scorched earth that [craft brewers] have repopulated and re-inhabited."

In most industries, companies are cheered when a larger firm buys them out. It means that they made a difference, that their product was valued and that they hopefully made a lot of money and achieved a little piece of the American dream. But the craft beer industry has always been different. It has always represented rebellion, and, as such, breweries are typically lauded for remaining independent—for not selling out.

"Craft brewers, for whatever reason, feel this is a unique industry and they are unique in their approach to what business means and how it works," says Odell Brewing cofounder Wynne Odell. "Buyouts don't fit with the culture of craft beer."

As a result, when AB InBev bought Breckenridge, the longtime Colorado brewery simply became "a brand" in Odell's point of view, "not a brewery." Breckenridge could still make great beer and it could still provide customers with a local experience, but the buyout changed the fundamental nature of what it was offering. Odell isn't dismissive, and she's not judgmental, but "there is a disconnect, and I think that is meaningful to a lot of people," she adds—very meaningful.

Some longtime friends ended up turning their backs on Usry and other Breckenridge executives. Others would only admit friendship privately. It was a tough new reality for people who had given everything to an industry they loved.

For some employees, though, the sale was simply an opportunity to make more and better beer, to have access to the resources of a giant company, more stable employment and consistent health and employee benefits. While some Breckenridge fans complained, many others felt the change was a good thing—both for the company and for the beer. Indeed, shortly after the merger, Breckenridge began turning out some of the most interesting beers it had made in years, adding more modern, fuller-flavored styles and updating its brands.

For Todd Usry and Todd Thibault, the buyout was simply a reality. Whatever their personal feelings, the two Todds, along with many other longtime Breckenridge employees, dove into the new situation with a vengeance. This had been their baby, after all. They had raised it and nurtured it, and now they wanted to do everything they could to protect its name.

That proved difficult to do with their colleagues, however.

In addition to Breckenridge losing its voting rights in the Brewers Association, the Breckenridge sale helped cause a huge rift inside the Colorado Brewers Guild, which had been founded in 1995 to promote and protect craft brewers and advocate for them in the state legislature.

In June 2016, after months of closed-door arguing, fourteen guild members left the organization to form their own brewery group. The mutineers included four of the state's largest craft breweries: New Belgium, Oskar Blues, Left Hand and Odell. They cited frustration with the guild's leadership as well as the fact that Breckenridge was still allowed to be a member.

While Breckenridge had been an important and supportive part of Colorado's craft beer scene for many years, many brewery owners believed that AB InBev was trying to force craft brewers to the side by using its might when it came to sales and distribution. They also felt like big beer had the ability to control and manipulate the companies that supply ingredients and equipment to beermakers. That situation became even more dangerous after the acquisitions because it gave AB InBev the ability to offer a lineup of former craft breweries to placate bars and restaurants that wanted them. The result, they believe, is that there will be fewer opportunities for independent craft breweries to get tap handles at those restaurants and bars.

Usry disagreed, and he and an AB InBev executive issued a statement about the Guild situation:

> First and foremost, we both respect the Brewers Association and all of the state brewers' guilds across the country. Some have shifted to drawing a line in the sand when it comes to independent breweries. From our viewpoint, this is divisive rhetoric and a distraction on what should really matter, namely the desire of all brewers to continue driving beer forward, both here in Colorado and across the country.
>
> Beer as a whole needs direction, and our mutual perspective is we need to focus on the challenges facing our category, together. With all of the noise the past few days, a key point that has been overlooked is a willingness to work together as a community. All of us make our living in the beer industry and, we hope, love drinking great beer. From that foundation, only together through passion and providing the best experiences can we move past the divisiveness and discuss a path forward that is inclusive, not exclusive.

After several months of negotiations, the members of the guild eventually voted to disband the original bylaws and reform under a united Brewers Guild with new leadership and with a new clause that didn't allow corporate-owned breweries to be members. They also hired a new executive and formed a new board of directors.

As a result of the buyout, Breckenridge no longer participates in as many industry events as it used to, including the Great American Beer Festival. But the brewery continues to grow and give back to Colorado, hosting events, supporting local artists and charities and making good beer.

Ironically, New Belgium sold out to Japanese beer giant Kirin in 2019, meaning that the state's largest brewery will no longer be eligible to participate in the guild starting in 2020. Avery Brewing, meanwhile, sold to Mahou San Miguel, an enormous Spanish conglomerate, ending its independence as well.

20

DENVER BEER CULTURE TODAY

When Laura Bruns and her brother, Chris Bruns, opened Factotum Brewhouse in 2015, their goal was to provide a community-focused oasis where homebrewers and other like-minded folks could come together over a beer—and even share and brew their recipes in the back.

Located on a residential street in Denver's Sunnyside neighborhood, Factotum is very small, and it produces only a few hundred barrels of beer per year. On any given day, you can find a food truck—a mainstay of brewery culture these days—parked outside and a range of people inside, from twenty-something hipsters to local families and beer geeks. They come looking to try whatever is new or to order a few pints of an old favorite. The same scene is repeated dozens and dozens of times at neighborhood breweries all over the metro area.

To start the business, the Brunses had to bootstrap the operation themselves. They didn't have big investors or loans, just their credit cards. That's the way a lot of craft breweries, going all the way back to the late 1980s, got started—and it worked out for a while. But things have changed.

"The old adage that you have to have money to make money is true," says Laura, who works full-time as a high school math and science teacher. "We were one of the last breweries in Denver to open with our own money and not with big shiny investors. At this point, I can walk into any brewery anywhere in the United States and tell you immediately if they started with a lot of money or if they bootstrapped it." Some of the bootstrappers have since closed.

"I see plenty of breweries out there with shit beer, but they are still open," Laura explains. "On the other hand, there are some good ones that have closed. The real difference is numbers sense. If you don't have it, that's where you will go wrong. And that is what gave me confidence. I looked around and said, 'If that person can make it work, then so can I.' You also have to be open to having a frank conversation about your weaknesses, about where you need help."

Factotum is a tiny business and a drop in the bucket when it comes to the overall beer market. But the Brunses aren't alone. In 2018, Colorado's 396 breweries generated an economic impact of more than $3 billion, and the state ranked first nationwide in economic impact per persons, according to the Brewers Association. Breweries provided more than 7,000 direct jobs (U.S. Census Bureau numbers recorded around 5,300 in 2016) and many more indirectly.

By mid-2019, there were closer to 420 craft breweries producing more than 1.5 million barrels a year, and the economic impact only increased. Only Pennsylvania, which has more than twice as many people as Colorado, and California, which has eight times as many people, brew more craft beer. And only California has a higher number of breweries. Add that to the massive Coors and AB InBev plants, which produce more beer than all of Colorado's independent breweries combined, and Colorado is truly one of the most important beer-producing states in the nation.

"That impact is a real part of our DNA in Colorado. It's not a fad and it's not going away," says Steve Kurowski, a longtime craft beer industry professional who served as the marketing and operations director of the Colorado Brewers Guild for a decade. But why Colorado? How did beer become such big business in a landlocked island of a state, far from either of the trend-setting coasts? The answers aren't entirely clear, but Kurowski has a few theories.

It started in 1873 when Adolph Coors found fresh springs in Golden and opened his brewery there. The family was so proud of it that they hyped that Rocky Mountain Spring water in their ads, and over time, Coors, which was only available in eleven states from 1933 until the late 1970s, became highly sought after, despite the fact that it was very similar in flavor and appearance to Bud, Miller, Pabst, Schlitz and any number of other light industrial lagers available in the 1960s, '70s and '80s.

Coors would argue that it was the quality, but the *New York Times* called it something else. "It is not so much the product as the mystique surrounding it that is fascinating," the newspaper wrote in a legendary article from December 28, 1975.

Former Colorado Brewers Guild spokesman Steve Kurowski. *Dustin Hall/The Brewtography Project.*

The *Times* continued,

> It seems to have won a reputation as the elixir of beers, the brew of Presidents, a prize to be smuggled into the East the way Americans abroad used to smuggle in contraband copies of Henry Miller's novels. Paul Newman, the king of beer-drinking actors, is said to require Coors on ice at all his movie sets. Henry Kissinger regularly brought cases back to Washington each time he made a trip to California. Secret Service agents were forbidden to bring extra crates aboard Federal planes after one agent was discovered to have loaded 38 cases onto a recent flight from the West Coast.
>
> Bootleggers from New Jersey to Tennessee regularly sell cases of Coors for as much as $15—about three times the Colorado retail price. (And three times what a New Yorker may pay for that favorite of Met fans, Schaefer.) Obviously, Coors must be a magic potion, not simply a fermented blend of barley malt, rice, hops and "Pure Rocky Mountain Spring Water."

College kids and Coors lovers east of the Mississippi River (where Coors wasn't available) would load up their car trunks with six packs during those decades and drive it back home—a practice that only intensified with the release of 1977's *Smokey and the Bandit*, in which a rich guy pays Burt Reynolds's character to smuggle Coors from Texas to Alabama.

Coors created a cult beer and "it set the table for craft beer," Kurowski says. "They said Colorado was unique, that we have something special here, whether it's in the water or not. That still lives in our psyche, whether people realize it or not."

Even more important, however, were Colorado's laws. After Prohibition, lawmakers who remembered the undue influence that breweries had exerted on the saloons they owned, created a system in which manufacturers had to sell to wholesalers who would then sell their beers to liquor stores and restaurants. This three-tier system, as it is known, exists in most other states as well and is designed to prevent corruption—but also to collect a lot of taxes.

Colorado lawmakers in the 1930s also prohibited breweries, wholesalers and saloon or restaurant owners from owning one another. In other words, a brewery couldn't own a wholesaler or a bar, and a bar couldn't own a wholesaler. More importantly for the microbreweries that would come later, though, was a provision that prohibited people or companies from owning more than one liquor store at a time.

This may have been put into place to prevent the mob, which had controlled the liquor trade during Prohibition, from retaining its power over the industry.

But in 1990s, when microbreweries were just getting started, it meant that Kim Jordan from New Belgium or Eric Wallace from Left Hand could walk into any liquor store they wanted and sell directly to the beer buyer. They didn't have to negotiate contracts with chain liquor outlets, groceries and convenience stores, as breweries did in other states.

"Those independent liquor stores really helped a lot of brewers get off the ground, and as a result we have more than the average number of packaging breweries," Kurowski says.

Another rule that helped breweries get a leg up in Colorado is one that allows small breweries that only sell beer in Colorado to distribute that beer themselves. That means they don't have to spend money to hire a distributor or deal with that second tier. Brewpubs, which also sell food, can also sell directly to consumers and can self-distribute.

More importantly for the recent craft beer boom, the fact that breweries here can open taprooms without selling food—something that Kevin Delange of Dry Dock Brewing pioneered in 2005—paved the way for the taproom culture. Other states, Kurowski says, are much more restrictive.

Grocery stores gained the right to sell full-strength beer in Colorado in 2019. *Jonathan Shikes.*

And finally, the Brewers Association is located in Boulder. "That didn't mean much nationally, though, until the Great American Beer Festival became the epicenter of the world of beer for five days a year," Kurowski explains, something that evolved slowly. "No other city gets that kind of attention. No other state. It put us on the map as being a great beer town before we truly were a great beer town."

As always, though, times are changing.

"Ten years ago, Colorado beer was needed in the rest of the country," Kurowski says. That's why packaging breweries like New Belgium, Odell and Great Divide were able to expand so quickly. But that's not the case anymore. Colorado's footprint is smaller now that regional powerhouse breweries have taken its place in many states. "Tasting rooms will be the main profit center in Colorado going forward. A lower percentage of breweries will package and sell on shelves."

That dynamic has become even more acute since the state did away with its long-standing regulations prohibiting chain stores from selling full-strength beer. More than likely, only a few packaging breweries will win in that very statistical game.

Today, Denver's beer scene is "super diverse" when it comes to styles and genres, Kurowski says. While some cities boast that excellence is a few styles, Denver makes world-class beer in many styles: sours, West Coast IPAs, German-style lagers—and even Czech and Polish styles—Belgian styles and East Coast IPAs. There are also breweries that specialize in spontaneously fermented beers, English-style cask ales, pre-Columbian corn-based chicha, Mexican-inspired beers, wine and whiskey barrel–aged beers, herb- and spice-inspired beers and beer/wine hybrids. "With seventy-plus breweries in the city, you're going to find something great—and they are only going to get better," he adds.

Is seventy breweries too many? Kurowski doesn't think so. "The neighborhoods will support neighborhood breweries. Hyper-local becomes very important. It's like restaurants. When one closes, another one opens, with a new idea or a new direction or a new concept."

One area where Denver's brewing world isn't so diverse, however, is in its people. The overwhelming majority of brewery owners and employees are white, and they are mostly men.

And this has always been the case, going back to the 1850s.

Luckily, those numbers have started to change—more quickly for women and more slowly for people of color. In 2010, there were fewer than ten women working as brewers in the entire state. While women worked in other brewery departments, primarily sales and taprooms, and some were co-owners, there's weren't many of them in other parts of the building.

Nearly ten years later, there are more than 150 women working statewide on brewhouse floors. Many more can also be found in brewery labs and on packaging lines. They are prominent in graphic design, marketing, sales, service, operations and management.

"People don't realize how many women are involved in the industry, which can be frustrating," says Factotum's Laura Bruns. Still, she acknowledges that the public faces of many small and popular Colorado breweries are still primarily male.

When, it comes to racial diversity, things are even worse. Anecdotal surveys show that only one brewery in the state, Denver's Novel Strand Brewing, has black ownership.

Latino representation was almost as stagnant until about 2017. There are now ten or so breweries with Latino ownership statewide. They include Novel Strand Brewing, Cheluna Brewing, Atrevida Brewing, Dos Luces Brewing, Coal Mine Avenue Brewing, Boggy Draw Brewery, Lady Justice Brewing, Raíces Brewing, Jade Mountain Brewing, Los Dos Potrillos, and Donovan Brewing (owned by former Blue Moon executive Keith Villa and his family).

Factotum co-owner Laura Bruns (*second from left*) with the owners of Lady Justice. *Factotum Brewhouse.*

A lack of diversity among brewery employees—and craft beer drinkers—isn't unique to Colorado, though, as the Brewers Association finally realized in 2018 when it brought on J. Nikol Jackson-Beckham, a university professor and PhD as its first diversity ambassador. Jackson-Beckham now travels the country to talk about ways in which craft breweries can diversify both their customer bases and their staffs.

Factotum is on the leading edge of that cause. When Bruns realized that many women were confused about beer styles and shy about ordering, she decided to begin offering women-only beer education classes. They fill up every time. Then, in 2018, she welcomed the owners of another small brewery, Lady Justice Brewing, to share Factotum's space. Lady J, which is owned by three women (one of whom is Latina), donates all of its profits to charities that provide opportunities and assistance to women and girls. (Lady Justice moved out in 2019.)

"I'm a teacher, so I know how to design a curriculum," Bruns says about her classes. "After we opened, I noticed that women who came into the brewery were almost bashful or embarrassed when they ordered a beer, so I would ask them what else they drink to try to get an idea for what they like," she explains. "Then I would let them try something, and usually I was right. What was most concerning, though, was how timid they were in the asking.

"My classes really stemmed from that. I wanted women to be able to go in any brewery anywhere in the whole world and know what ABV is and IBUs, and to know where their palate is and be able to narrow it down. Then ask questions. They are consumers, too, and can be part of the craft scene and enjoy this product without being left out."

21

MODERN INNOVATORS

When "award-winning homebrewer" Sean Buchan opened Cerebral Brewing in late 2015, he heard a familiar, disdainful refrain from some of Denver's beer geeks. It went like this:

"The scariest words in any description of a new craft brewery: 'award-winning homebrewer.' They're not all terrible, but there are quite a few that won't survive. Someday they'll refer to this as the Great Colorado Brew Rush, when every homebrewer and his brother-in-law thought they could make it big."

In fact, those were the exact words that one commenter used after a story about Cerebral appeared in *Westword*, Denver's alternative weekly newspaper.

In retrospect, the comment sounds ludicrous. Buchan, who has developed a thick skin since then, may not have had any professional experience before opening Cerebral on busy Colfax Avenue, but he's turned the brewery into one of the hottest, most lauded destinations in Denver and a must-visit spot for beer tourists coming in from out of town.

Like most people who do something different, something innovative, whether it was leasing space in a downtrodden neighborhood, like Wynkoop Brewing did in 1988, or bottling Belgian beer like New Belgium did in the early '90s, or focusing entirely on wood-aged sour ales, like Crooked Stave did in 2011, Buchan—and his beer—were criticized.

He admits to some nerves beforehand. After all, some of the other breweries with planned openings that same year included Bierstadt Lagerhaus, owned by Bill Eye, one of the most decorated and respected professional brewers in the city; Spangalang Brewing, whose ownership included longtime Great

Cerebral Brewing owner Sean Buchan. *Cerebral Brewing.*

Divide head brewer Taylor Rees and probrewers Austin Wiley and Darren Boyd; Ratio Beerworks, helmed by Jason zumBrunnen, a journeyman brewer who'd studied the art of beermaking at both the Seibel Institute in Chicago and Doemens Academy in Munich, Germany; and Call to Arms Brewing, founded by a trio of Avery Brewing vets with twenty years combined experience in the industry.

"It was all ex-pros," he says. "It was terrifying."

For the first six months, Buchan let it affect the styles he brewed because he was afraid to make the unusual beers that had drawn him to brewing in the first place. But after that, he settled in and began focusing on the styles that made him happy. One of those was a style that the Brewers Association now calls "juicy" or "hazy" pale ales and IPAs. Pioneered primarily in Vermont, New Hampshire and Massachusetts, juicy IPAs are typically loaded with hops, but unlike American, or West Coast, IPAs, they have very low bitterness, which makes them more appealing to some people. The lack of bitterness is a result of the hops being added to the wort after it has cooled rather than while it is boiling with the malted barley. This process is known as dry hopping.

Because of this, and because of the yeast strains that juicy IPA makers choose, the proteins in the hops bind to the yeast, giving the beer a hazy appearance. Some people believe this also creates more intensity in flavor and aroma. While the appearance is a joy to some people, it is anathema to others, who believe the only good beer is a clear beer. That's because when microbreweries were getting their start in the '80s and '90s, some were unfiltered, or just poorly made, giving them a hazy appearance—an association that has been hard for many old-school brewers to shake. Homebrewers, too, often make hazy beer, which is a sign to some of unprofessionalism. And while the process that Buchan and his peers used is actually planned out and heavily designed, the anti-hazers confuse it with poorly made beer.

Either way, the style swept from the East Coast to the rest of the country in 2016 and 2017, becoming so popular that the BA eventually added three categories for it in 2018 and a fourth in 2019.

Buchan was right on trend without meaning to be, and although it took three years, his passion was eventually validated by the powers that be at the BA—not that he was waiting around. By 2017, Cerebral was already working with other innovative breweries, both in Colorado and in other states, to learn more about the chemistry behind their beers. Locally, these included Weldwerks Brewing in Greeley, Odd13 Brewing in Lafayette, Outer Range Brewing in Frisco, Fiction Beer Company in Denver and New Image Brewing in Arvada.

Like Adam Avery at Avery Brewing in 1993, Kevin DeLange at Dry Dock in 2005 and Tim Myers at Strange Craft Beer Company in 2010, Buchan was a homebrewer, and he used that to his advantage when it came time to open his own place. "As a homebrewer, I could brew whatever I wanted to, with no style restrictions, no restrictions at all," he says. "I used that as my inspiration. If I liked to drink it, other people might want to as well."

So, who is pushing boundaries in Denver now? Buchan has a short list that includes TRVE Brewing with their techniques and unusual taproom, Comrade Brewing with its use of hops, Ratio Beerworks with its style and market-savvy and Bierstadt Lagerhaus with its single-minded dedication to sixteenth-century German lagers. Outside of Denver, he notes Weldwerks, Outer Range, Cellar West Artisan Ales and Cannonball Creek Brewing.

While some older breweries like New Belgium, Avery, Left Hand and Odell continue to innovate when it comes to science, technology and research, "the young breweries are pushing the scene. Yes, you can say that everything has been done before, but there are always new or different ways to look at things."

It's probably not a surprise that former Colorado Brewers Guild marketing director Steve Kurowski's list looks very similar to Buchan's. And so does that of Drew Watson, who opened Hops & Pie Artisan Pizzeria and Craft Brew Taproom with his wife, Leah, in 2010.

"It takes a lot to stand out today," says Watson. There are so many breweries looking for handles at his bar, in fact, that Watson had to stop doing tastings. "As a chef, if you make something and people don't like it, it hurts a little bit. Since I know that, I just can't bring myself to taste their beer and give them feedback. Too many just aren't very good." Instead, Watson keeps his ear to the ground, listens to friends and customers whose opinions he respects, reads the beer media and seeks out the beers and breweries that people are talking about.

In Denver, that list includes Station 26 Brewing, Ratio Beerworks, Hogshead Brewery, Call to Arms Brewing, TRVE Brewing and Bierstadt Lagerhaus. Outside of the city, he looks for beers from Casey Brewing and Blending, Outer Range Brewing, Cannonball Creek Brewing, Weldwerks Brewing and Westbound & Down Brewing.

The Watsons have been in business since before most of the city's breweries at this point, so they have watched the scene grow and change.

"You go back a few years and there was so much passion. People were giving up their high-priced tech jobs and taking out second mortgages because they loved it," he says. "Today, though, there is more bad beer than good, and people are jumping in for the wrong reasons."

The same is true for some of his customers. "People are seeking whales, they are looking for what is hot instead of what is good. If you go back four years, the sours and the barrel-aged beers that people were coveting were intense. They were flavorful beers that were full of nuances on a lot of levels. Today, they are looking for drinkable beers that are simple, bright and juicy. They are rookie beers that people who are new to the hobby can enjoy right away. A lot of them are delicious, but it's different. The appreciation is just different," he says.

So, who are the city's innovators? Here is a list of some of the great ones.

TRVE Brewing

TRVE Brewing opened in 2011 in a narrow space in a former art gallery. Pronounced like *true*, it takes its aesthetic from Scandinavian death metal.

TRVE features saisons, wood and wine barrel–aged wild and sour ales named after death metal bands and songs. Like the name, owner Nick Nunns has remained true to himself and his mission since the beginning. The taproom is dark, the beer club was capped at 666 members and there is a goat-skull altar and a sign in the bathroom that reads, "Employees Must Carve Slayer into Forearms Before Returning to Work." TRVE turns out delicious beers without pandering to trends or tastes, small-batch sour and wild ales in particular.

Comrade Brewing

Colorado breweries have been making delicious IPAs for a long time, but there are a lot of people who would say that by the early 2010s, some of them had begun to taste more like the 1990s. Enter Comrade Brewing, where owner David Lin and head brewer Marks Lanham focus on newer hop varieties. One of the first beers out of the gate was Superpower IPA, and it has since come to define the high-IBU, West Coast–style beers brewed in Colorado.

Denver Beer Company

One of the first taproom-only breweries in Denver, DBC's original aim was to continually make new beers without ever repeating—like a chef producing seasonal dishes. That didn't work out, in part because customers kept demanding their old favorites. But Denver Beer Company has paved the way as one of the most stylish breweries to open in a neighborhood that would explode with popularity, creating an unparalleled gathering spot. Run by two smart owners who are always ahead of the curve, the brewery eventually opened its own canning facility and later expanded with a second location and then a second brand called Cerveceria Colorado, which specializes in progressive politics and beers using Mexican ingredients.

Our Mutual Friend

An idealistic nanobrewery when it opened in the River North Arts District in 2012, OMF has grown from hipster hangout with inconsistent beer brewed on a one-barrel system into one of the most engaging, experimental and on-point beermakers in town. Boasting a homey feel that is one part dad's study and one part college apartment, OMF has a lovely patio and a special fondness for elegant Brett beers and wood barrel–aged saisons. The brewery, which continues to evolve, has turned its ideals into reality.

Ratio Beerworks embraces Denver's food truck culture. *Jonathan Shikes.*

Ratio Beerworks

Born out of a group of punk rockers turned dads, Ratio opened as one of the slickest, most well-thought-out breweries in town in 2015, carrying an artsy, musical vibe, a midcentury modern aesthetic and traditional beers that were almost all given an unusual twist. The brewery—which is always packed— has continued to turn out a great product, hosting interesting events, killer parties and keeping itself close to the punk edge.

River North Brewery

One of the first of a new breed of taprooms when it opened in 2012, River North Brewery also staked a claim to the name of Denver's hottest new neighborhood. But the brewery, founded by Matthew Hess, has also made consistently top-notch beer. Although it made its reputation with high-gravity Belgian beers and barrel-aged specialties, it has since expanded into other categories—and done them well. It also boasts one of the most mature and extensive barrel-aging programs in the state. In 2019, River North Brewery returned to its namesake neighborhood after being forced out three years earlier when its building was torn down.

Black Project Wild & Spontaneous

One of the "it" breweries for the past few years, not just in Colorado, but also nationwide, Black Project only makes beers that are spontaneously fermented with wild yeast and other microbes. The majority are sour and made with enormous amounts of fruit. On the cutting edge of spontaneous fermentation in the United States, Black Project was born out of a love for this style of beer and is still the only brewery doing what it does 100 percent of the time.

Bierstadt Lagerhaus

Innovation might be the wrong word to describe Bierstadt Lagerhaus, since owners Bill Eye and Ashleigh Carter, along with partner Chris Rippe, focus entirely on German-style Reinheitsgebot lagers. You won't find any added ingredients or trendy styles here. Rather, Eye and Carter own a pre–World War II brewhouse that they purchased in Germany, on which they make large quantities of a perfectly crafted pilsner, helles, dunkel and others.

Station 26 Brewing.

Founded in an old firehouse, complete with an old fire pole, Station 26 filled a geographical hole in Denver where there were no breweries—and it did so while making some of the best beer in Denver, in every category and just about every style. While some breweries are really good at one style or a couple, Station 26 nails them all. It shouldn't be a surprise, though. Owner Justin Baccary hired Wayne Waananen, who began his career at Vail's Hubcap Brewing and later helped create Blue Moon. Though Waananen has since departed, Station 26 has continued to excel, expanding its canned distribution and hopping on beer trends like milkshake IPAs and rose-style ales.

Outside of Denver, other modern innovators include:

Founded in Glenwood Springs in 2014 by Troy Casey, **Casey Brewing and Blending** focuses on wild and sour ales. Troy Casey's art comes not necessarily in the brewing but in aging his beers with yeast and bacteria and fruit and then blending them for specific flavors. He was one of the first to rely solely on Colorado-grown fruit and other ingredients.

Continually named one of best breweries in the state by both its fellow brewers and the public, **Cannonball Creek Brewing** in Golden focuses on immaculate, experimental IPAs and traditional styles, like porters and pilsners. The brewery perhaps epitomizes the idea of being happy being small, as the owners have no intention of expanding or packaging. They simply make great beer, over and over again.

Weldwerks Brewing exploded onto Colorado's beer scene in 2015 with Juicy Bits, its luscious New England–style IPA, just as the popularity of this style was beginning to take off. Since then, the Greeley brewery has pushed boundaries in all directions. Not only does it rely on its somewhat remote location in the town of the Greeley to push scarcity and demand, but it also spent one year brewing new beers each week, reaching more than 130 different ones. It has single-handedly changed tastes, trends, expectations and habits in Colorado.

BIBLIOGRAPHY

Abbott, Carl, Stephen J. Leonard and Thomas J. Noel. *Colorado: A History of the Centennial State*. Boulder: University Press of Colorado, 2013.

Acitelli, Tom. *The Audacity of Hops*. Chicago: Chicago Review Press, 2017

Banham, Russ. *Coors: A Rocky Mountain Legend*. Lyme, CT: Greenwich Publishing Group, 1988.

Bromwell, Henrietta. *Fiftyniners' Directory: Colorado Argonauts of 1858–1859*. Denver, CO: n.p., 1926.

Coel, Margaret, Jane Barker and Karen Gilleland. *The Tivoli: Bavaria in the Rockies*. Boulder: Colorado and West, 1985.

Hickenlooper, John W. *The Opposite of Woe: My Life in Beer and Politics*. New York: Penguin, 2016.

McLeod, Robert W. *Ghost Breweries of Colorado: A History of Centennial State Brewing*. Self-published: CreateSpace, 2016

Noel, Thomas J. *The City and the Saloon: Denver 1858–1916*. Boulder: University Press of Colorado, 1996.

Rochlin, Harriet, and Fred Rochlin. *Pioneer Jews: A New Life in the Far West*. Self-published: iUniverse, 2014.

Sealover, Ed. *Mountain Brew: A Guide to Colorado's Breweries*. Charleston, SC: The History Press, 2011.

Thomas, Dave. *Of Mines and Beer!: A History of Brewing in Nineteenth-Century Colorado and Beyond*. Self-published: CreateSpace, 2013.

Van Wieren, Dale P. *American Breweries II*. West Point, PA: Eastern Coast Breweriana, 1995.

INDEX

ABOUT THE AUTHOR

Jonathan Shikes is a Northwestern University–trained journalist with twenty-five years of experience as a writer, editor and manager at daily and weekly newspapers and websites. He has covered the craft beer industry in Colorado for more than a decade and is a frequent denizen of several local tap houses. He lives in Denver with his wife and two children.

Visit us at
www.historypress.com